Shattered and Restored

ELSA McINNES

Castle Publishing Ltd
Auckland
New Zealand

Shattered and Restored
Published by Castle Publishing Ltd
PO Box 68 800, Newton
Auckland, New Zealand

Ph: +64 9 378 4052
Fax: +64 9 376 3855
info@castlepublishing.biz
www.castlepublishing.biz

© Elsa McInnes 2003

ISBN 0-9582398-1-9

Production: Andrew Killick
Cover Design: Jeff Hagan

Cover photo: Gold-mining tailings, Naseby
(courtesy of Ernslaw One Ltd.)
Backcover: Elsa and family

Printed in New Zealand by Wentforth Print

First Published in 1990
by ANZEA Publishers, Australia
Reprinted 1991

All scripture quotations in this publication,
unless otherwise stated, are from
the Good News Translation – Second Edition
Copyright © 1992 by American Bible Society.
Used by Permission.

ALL RIGHTS RESERVED

No part of this publication may be reproduced,
stored in a retrieval system, or transmitted,
in any form or by any means, electronic, mechanical,
photocopying, recording, or otherwise,
without prior written permission from the publisher.

In memory of Garth
whose passion for God nurtured mine
and who shared the journey with me
as my husband and best friend.

FOREWORD

I feel full of thanksgiving for this moving, humble, Christ-centred book. In telling her own story and making herself so vulnerable, Elsa McInnes has made three remarkable achievements: she has helped those of us who have not been asked to walk through 'the valley of the shadow of death' to catch a glimpse of how it feels to be there, she has shown how we might best help those who find themselves facing, through death, the loss of a much-loved partner and she has testified to the fact that God does bring treasures out of this darkness.

But that is not to say that this book provides easy, take-away answers nor that it is shallow or triumphalistic. On the contrary, it is real. That is what makes it so moving and so strangely joyful.

The book, I believe, will strengthen the bereaved, especially when the tunnel of grief appears to have no end. It will inform and encourage Christian helpers and it will be cherished by those who need to be reminded of the truth of Romans 8 – that absolutely nothing can separate us from the love of God.

I count it a privilege to have had a brief encounter with the author during my first visit to New Zealand and to have been invited to recommend this book. I do this whole-heartedly with the conviction that through its pages healing will flow from God to those who read it.

Joyce Huggett

CONTENTS

Preface	11
Acknowledgements	14
1. My World Broke in the Night	17
2. From Trust, Through Turmoil, to Trust Again	27
3. Rejected Love	35
4. He Sets the Captives Free	45
5. He Comforts All Who Mourn	49
6. My Will, Not Yours, Be Done	59
7. Come On Out	73
8. Please Jesus, Don't Die	85
9. Promise of Restoration	91
10. The Empty Tomb	99
11. When Darkness Seems For Ever	107
12. In Two Minds	121
13. Give Me Your Cloak	133
14. With Love from God	153
15. The Morning Chorus	165
Epilogue	177
References	186

PREFACE

This book is written to encourage those who through tragedy have lost their faith in God. It grew out of the tragedy that shook my world five years ago when my husband died suddenly. Over and over again the words 'your faith will sustain you' were either spoken or written by well meaning friends. Inside my heart cried out, 'What faith?' It had exploded along with my world.

Few will admit to shattered faith. They feel vulnerable and seldom disclose their struggle to fellow Christians whom they suspect will not understand. I write to encourage those who struggle with very real faith issues and who ask as I did, 'Where is God?' 'If he is powerful and loving why did he let this happen to me?' 'How can I hear God above my raging emotions?' I want to encourage those who are confused because a faith, once strong and vibrant, now feels hollow and empty. Familiar words bounce off the walls of their hearts leaving only desolation and more hurt because such words are no longer sustaining.

Two years of my own personal struggle preceded the writing of this book. It may never have been written had not God planted a seed in my spirit in the form of a throwaway comment by my brother-in-law. 'Write a book' was his casual comment to me when I was mulling over the question of what to fill the year with apart from parenting.

Until Garth died I had no concept of how pathetic my attempts to help two young widows had been. I had not begun to understand them. I didn't know the powerful pull to end life until I myself felt utterly worthless and alone. It wasn't until my faith lay in pieces that I discovered the crucial role the church family plays in being 'Jesus with skin on', reflecting the love, acceptance and affirmation of God, especially to those who blame God or who struggle with deep anger at a senseless death.

The book grew within me. It began to take shape. I knew it must address the issue of a wounded faith; it must give helpers a way to get inside the skin of those in pain, to understand and respond more appropriately; it must show the church family the wonderful opportunity they have to reflect the heart of Jesus to those who question his love. Clearly the book had to be autobiographical. But writing my own story is costly. It is a vulnerable position yet a deep privilege. My story is written not to tell the world how it was for me but because I know other people hurt as I hurt, ask the questions I asked and hunger to know that they are not alone, and to believe that God can, indeed will, restore their faith and hope.

I wrote when hope had been restored, but I wrote especially to touch those who, maybe right now, are in that dark place where pain has robbed them even of their faith; who cry with Jesus, 'My God, why have you abandoned me?' I want to encourage those who no longer believe there is a God to cry to – at least not the one they knew and trusted. Yet God is faithful. I have found him so. He is alive and active and *will* bring them through the darkness into the glorious light of his presence with joy.

If I have one plea to make to those bereft of God, it is 'keep communicating'. Restoration is possible where communication remains open. These last five years have shown me three things that enhance communication with God, and my story will illustrate these.

Firstly, the recognition that a love relationship with Jesus will involve *all* the emotions found in a deeply satisfying human relationship. There will be both trust and mistrust, love and anger, hope and fear. I've learned the importance of being real about all of it with Jesus. Secondly, I've discovered that Jesus also expresses his relationship to me in a wide variety of ways. At times he embraces me in love. I've experienced deep comfort and felt his tears. At other times he has challenged me or gently rebuked. When I limited his expression I limited our relationship. I'm more open now to be surprised by him.

Finally, the desperation to hear him led me to explore new, yet old, prayer possibilities. In the book I have shared some of my experiences of such meetings with Jesus. They are very personal and I counted the cost. But if one reader is helped by exploring the possibilities of meeting and relating to Jesus in similar life changing ways, I will be glad.

I'm very aware of my limited understanding of the mystery of God and the impossibility of trying to wrap in a bundle of ordinary words that which I have come to appreciate so deeply – God's faithfulness and incredible love. My prayer is that God will take this imperfect work and still use it to his glory to encourage those who are disillusioned in their faith. I believe God's desire is to show that the words spoken by his prophet, Isaiah, and reiterated by his Son, Jesus, still convey the truth of his ministry today.

> He brings good news to the poor.
> He heals the broken hearted.
> He announces release to the captives.
> The time has come when the Lord will save his people.
> He comforts all who mourn.
> He gives joy and gladness instead of grief. It is true today…
> He WILL rebuild what has been in ruins.

Elsa McInnes

ACKNOWLEDGEMENTS

I'm most grateful to my Lord, and the many faithful people who have shaped my life because they loved him and touched me with that love.

Garth who, more than any other, helped me grow in God and gave me rich companionship along the way.

My children for their continuing affirmation of me and the wonderful companionship they offer as young adults. For their permission to include some of their story as it intertwines with mine.

My Nan for first introducing me to Jesus. My Mum and sisters for unconditional love and acceptance through my negative times.

St Paul's church family for their practical tangible support and love to us all over the years.

Margaret Schrader for her gentle spiritual guidance following Garth's death which kept the buried seed of my faith warm till it could sprout again.

Joyce Huggett for her wisdom born of God and without whose practical assistance about writing I would surely have floundered. For her positive endorsement in the foreword.

Leonie, for introducing me to Joyce, for our deep friendship, her belief in me and for our special times of prayer over many years now.

Margery and Ron Newman for always offering a warm welcome and lunch at 'Shiloh', a quiet place where I wrote much of the first edition.

Others for helping in the birth of this book. My brother-in-law, Harvey, for casually uttering the words, 'write a book', those who faithfully prayed

Acknowledgements

through the labour and delivery of this book and Esther Loader for typing up my messy script for the first edition.

Ron Hart for trimming, punctuating and rephrasing the original manuscript with skill, sensitivity and humour, and Lorraine Inskeep and Ron Hart for painstaking attention to proofreading this second edition.

Lorraine Inskeep for her special friendship, prayer and sustained encouragement to keep writing about my journey with God

Andrew Killick, production manager at Castle Publishing, for editing the epilogue and overseeing this new edition.

One word applies to all these people: encouragers. Encouragement is a priceless gift and I want to offer my thanks to these and all others who have offered me a warm hand on my journey.

chapter

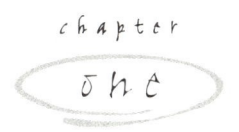

one

MY WORLD BROKE IN THE NIGHT

19 March 1985, 9.30 p.m. is indelibly printed on my mind. At that exact moment my world exploded. Thus began the longest, hardest work in my life – reassembling the broken pieces and the shattered fragments of my faith.

At 9.00 p.m. that night I said goodnight to my parents and joined my husband, Garth, in bed. My heart was glad. It had been a wonderful day like so many in the past three months while Garth was off work and receiving treatment for cancer. The day had been full of precious moments. Garth had washed the car and as I watched him I felt a pull to join him. We worked together, then sat in the sun and peeled pears. He had potted a few ferns and then busied himself preparing a sound system for the visit of Bill and Delores Winders to our parish. We had shared lunch in the garden with the background twitter of friendly fantails and the rustle of leaves approaching autumn. I had shared with Garth a recent part of my journey with the Lord – the wonderful freedom and wholeness the Lord had brought to me. He had remade moments from the past and set me free from a crippling fear of rejection. Together we shared the joy.

The afternoon had passed in happy preparation for the visit of my parents who were flying up to stay for a week or two. I had met them at the airport. Garth had chosen to stay home and supervise tea. We shared a meal amid joyful chatter, catching up on family news. Mum and Dad were relieved to see Garth looking well and entering conversation with vigour and humour. The children had much to tell also, and before they went to bed we phoned my sister, Valerie. We confirmed the safe arrival of Mum and Dad and wished Colin, her son, a happy twenty-first birthday.

By 9.00 p.m. we were all tired. With those warm memories I joined Garth in the bedroom and rubbed his aching back and prayed for him. I asked God to pour the love from my heart through my finger tips into his body and to continue to heal him. While I was gently massaging his back he began to cough, but with the coughing came blood; a little at first and then a lot. He rose and headed to the bathroom. I was by his side seeing, yet not believing. With horror I watched helplessly his struggle to breathe. My stomach knotted at the battle taking place before my eyes.

I don't remember how I found our doctor's phone number. I shook violently and it seemed an eternity before the beeps stopped and Rob answered. I was praying, 'Hurry, Rob, please hurry', and desperately wanting to be back with Garth in his struggle for life. In a daze I said, 'Rob, Garth's bleeding and he can't breathe. Please come now.' I believe I almost shouted at him. Perhaps I did because later I realised something had woken the children.

Rob's measured tones and gentle voice live with me still. 'I think he needs more help than I can give him.'

'But will you come?' I pleaded desperately, even as his words confirmed my own deep fears.

'I'll come right away,' he promised. I dropped the phone and raced back to be with Garth. Barely a minute had passed, I suppose, in that conversation which seemed to take an eternity.

Garth was battling for life and losing fast. In my anguish I cried out to God. I don't know what I said. It was torn from the depth of my being as I pleaded for his life.

By 9.30 it was all over. Garth's struggle had ceased and he slid unconscious to the floor in a pool of blood, and the bottom dropped out of my world. I was helpless to do anything. I couldn't resuscitate him.

My World Broke in the Night

I could do nothing, absolutely nothing, but every cell within me screamed out to do something. I recoiled from every detail of that scene even as it etched itself indelibly on my mind.

Rob arrived at my side, his arm around me as I knelt by Garth. He made no move towards Garth. I knew it was no use anyway. I said, without tears, what I already knew. 'He's dead, isn't he?'

Rob confirmed it with a quiet 'Yes. I'm really sorry.' His arm was firm upon my shoulder.

Somewhere in those moments I became aware that the children, or at least some of them, were up and moving about and that the local ambulance officers were also present. My fuzzy mind struggled with that. Rob must have rung them. He must have known. I was still reliving the last moments of struggle. Hammering away in my head were the words: 'He's dead. He's dead.' But there was an impenetrable wall between my head and my heart. I knew and yet I didn't.

I found myself thinking of the impact all this would have on my children's lives. I turned to the boys' room to find Ian kneeling by his bed, obviously pleading with God for his Daddy's life, and Jim, wide-eyed, sitting on his bed. So they had been aware. How much had they seen? Somehow I told them the truth and held them while they took it in. Many thoughts flashed through my mind as I stroked their blonde hair and hugged them tight.

'They didn't even get to say goodbye ... It's all too sudden ... They're not ready for it, Lord ... It's too much ... They prayed believing you would heal him. What have you done to their faith? ... What does the future hold for them? ... How can these fourteen-year-olds grow into manhood in a healthy way without a father? ... I can't give them the male model they need ... God, what have you done?!'

With questions, accusations and mixed emotions churning within, I went to the girls' room where, half an hour before, they had contentedly fallen asleep. Aneta, eight years old, was awake, her long, blonde hair tousled on the pillow, her eyes big and frightened. 'Daddy's dead, isn't he,' she said. She knew. We wrapped ourselves together as if trying to shut out the pain and she cried a little. I still didn't. The blessed anaesthetic of

19

shock had taken over – God's gift, I believe, when the inner spirit has had all it can take without breaking. There would be weeks and months of painful grief ahead. Right now the numbing allowed me to function, to reach beyond myself to the needs of my children and others. I could function with amazing clarity. God knows we need to at such times and he has provided the mechanism of shock just for that enabling. Later, I would crash. Later, I would not be able to think straight or to see beyond my pain. But right then I could, and I thanked God.

I moved across to Katrina's bed and looked down at her peaceful, sleeping form. She was only ten. I was glad she hadn't seen him. I hated myself for having to shatter her world. I woke her and the look in my eyes must have said it all. She looked deep inside me in silence and then said, 'It's Daddy. Isn't it?'

'Yes, honey, he's dead.' She began to shake. No words, no tears, just a silent shaking that continued until 2.00 a.m. when we finally crawled back to bed.

Rob asked me if I would like to see Garth, now laid on our bed. Uncertain, yet driven by inner need, I slipped into our room not knowing what I thought or felt. The moment I saw him a deep emptiness filled me. He was not there. I looked only at an empty shell – cold and white, drained of colour and warmth.

Suddenly a great lump rose in my throat. I had wanted to say goodbye. There had been no time. He couldn't speak in his struggle and now the chance was gone. I couldn't say goodbye to an empty shell. The man I loved and lived for was gone. I sat in silence thinking, 'I've heard it said, "People look sweet in death." It's not true. The real person isn't even here.' The emptiness engulfed me. Finally, with a heavy heart, I returned to the children. Aneta slipped in to see Garth though Jim warned, 'Don't. You won't like it.' How did he know? Had he seen him? I didn't know.

I remembered that my parents were still sound asleep in the front room, totally oblivious to all that was happening. I felt deeply for them. I slipped into their room, gently shook them and told them Garth was dead. I was like an observer at the scene, standing apart, reflecting on how they would feel having seen Garth so well forty minutes earlier.

The children slipped in behind me and curled up with Mum and Dad, desperately needing to be held, to be cuddled and to talk.

For the second time that night I phoned Valerie, shattering their birthday celebrations. In the forty minutes since the last phone call my world had fallen apart; nothing remained the same.

Yet in the days to come I was surprised how so much did remain the same. How could we still eat, sleep, wash dishes, clean clothes, bathe, brush teeth and meet people? How dare the world and life go on when Garth had died? How could people go shopping and chat at check-out counters? How could they stroll casually round town, involved in their own affairs as if nothing had happened? Didn't they know my husband had died? The world should hold its breath!

But life did go on even as we, who grieved, died inside. In time we learned, with God's help, to live again; to rejoin life. Part of the healing was in attending to the ordinary needs that marched relentlessly on when we wished they would stop. Life and its daily movement and demands were gifts from God, though I couldn't see it then.

Life for me had stopped in its tracks. Fortunately, Valerie responded immediately, offering to phone all the relevant people in the South Island. That was a mighty relief. Phoning her had been difficult enough and I still had the most important call to make – the call to Garth's parents. How I wished I could ease their pain for them. This was their eldest son, their first child. They now had the sad task of informing family and friends.

The ripples spread and I became aware of the effect of Garth's death on a widening circle of people. The parish needed to know. At 9.00 a.m. Bill and Delores Winder were commencing a healing seminar and ministry in our church. I was glad not to be in their place conducting a healing seminar in a church grieving for its minister with all the doubts and questions that would arise about God and faith, prayer and power. I had questions enough of my own!

Why, when God had, in the past, powerfully worked his healing through the Winders, did Garth die just on the eve of their arrival? It felt like a deliberate attempt by Satan to thwart God's plan for healing. If so, was the devil more powerful than God? Where was God? The Winders

Shattered and Restored

were going to preach the power and reality of a God who heals, and I believed all that. Yet my husband was dead. I believed in a God of love and power. Yet in this cruel and sudden death I saw no evidence of either. I desperately needed to know that God was still a God of love and power whom I could trust for my future, the children's future and for Garth's destiny.

Having informed the Session Clerk and the Jacksons (who were hosting the Winders), the wheels of human involvement continued to turn through the night. The Presbyterian Church network spread the news up and down the land. Meanwhile, I pulled my thoughts back to my family and joined my parents and children.

Each child reacted in a unique way to the blow so rudely dealt them. Ian talked incessantly. He reflected on Garth's ministry and how he saw it being fulfilled in the future. He needed desperately to see a continuity, something on-going from his Dad's life and work. Jim, Ian's twin brother, cried a little and expressed his ideas about funerals. Katrina continued to shake, and said little. Aneta just curled up with her Nan from which warm safe place she talked about her Dad and what she thought should happen at her Dad's funeral.

Sometime before midnight two precious parish elders left their warm beds and came to sit with us; empty of words but full of love. The shock of Garth's death triggered an asthma attack in Dad and I had to call Rob Cameron back in the early morning to relieve his distress. He came willingly. I was grateful for such a caring, Christian doctor.

Finally, at about 2.00 a.m., we went, reluctantly, to bed. There was comfort in being together and, instinctively, the children settled in my room. Little Aneta curled up with me in the double bed, her warm body snuggled in close. I lay wide awake, listening to the children's soft breathing. My mind was in a turmoil; the reality still dreamlike.

Aneta whispered in my ear, 'Mummy, have you prayed? I have.'

I ventured, 'Would you like to tell me what you prayed?'

Her answer left me stunned at the incredible understanding of a small child. 'I've written a love letter to Daddy in my mind and asked the angels to deliver it.'

I had not the understanding my little girl had. She understood the unbroken communication in the spirit with those we love who are in the Lord. As a little girl she had always broken through all barriers to reach her Dad. People taking his time and attention had never stopped her and rules had never stopped her. Once, at eighteen months old, she had left the house in the dark, slipped into the church next door and padded down the aisle in bare feet and pyjamas into her Daddy's arms in the middle of evening worship. She broke all the barriers he erected in his preoccupation with work, always managing to get his attention. And now, she would not allow even death to be a barrier to communication. She found a way. I still had not. I still grieved for unspoken goodbyes. In Garth's sudden death, I had sensed the Lord standing in the corner of the room welcoming him home, picking him up and taking him to himself. But I still had deep regrets because we didn't get a chance to say goodbye.

I lay awake at two o'clock in the morning; the only sound being the deep breathing of my sleeping children. Suddenly, I was aware of a presence in the room. The space was filled with the spirit of Garth. He was alive and rejoicing. He was so much at peace my spirit and heart leapt for joy and we communicated spirit to spirit in ways I would never have believed possible. We shared all we had wanted to say in those last ten minutes of Garth's life. The words were deep in our spirits, spoken and received simultaneously. When all was said, the presence faded and was gone and I was once again alone with the children. There was a deep peace in my heart. I knew that Garth was alive in joy with Jesus and I also knew that he had a deep peace about us. There are no words to describe what happened. It belongs to a different realm that is more real than what we normally think of as reality.

His obvious peace about us astounded me. 'He must know the pain we face,' I thought. 'How can he have such a peace about it?' I used to wonder how heaven could be such a blissful place if its inhabitants, like Christ, were aware of the suffering of loved ones on earth. A better description would be hell. Jim shared similar reservations. Yet in that experience of spiritual communion with Garth I knew his peace about it all. He had a new perspective; that of God himself.

I believe that on most issues God's perspective is totally different from ours:

> 'My thoughts,' says the Lord, 'are not like yours, and my
> ways are different from yours. As high as the heavens
> are above the earth, so high are my ways and thoughts
> above yours.' (Isaiah 55:8, 9)

His perspective of life and death, joy and pain, good and bad, loss and gain, cannot be compared with ours. He sees the whole and we see only a fraction; too small to grasp the pattern just as a little jigsaw piece is unidentifiable out of its context.

The peace I experienced at 2.00 a.m. was not the peace of wishful thinking that all would be smooth and calm, rather it was that, in spite of all we would still have to face, all *would* be well. Often in darkness, a year later, I reminded myself of that incredible experience and it helped me through days that, from my human perspective, were anything but well.

The peace that filled me at 2.00 a.m. remained and deepened into an enormous gratitude overriding and softening the pain. The force of the pain was still to be felt long and often, but this time was a time for thanks. So still wide awake at 5.00 a.m. I slipped silently out of bed and settled at the dining room table. I wrote in my prayer diary all the things for which I was deeply grateful. Perhaps subconsciously I knew that in the grief still to come I would forget the goodness of God and his gifts. I would even, in the future, challenge that he gave me anything. Instead, I would see him as the robber, the one who stole my love, quenched my joy, disillusioned my children and left me in pieces.

Right now, resting in God's peace, I needed to record this time of remembering so I might refer to it in the future (like the stone altars of the Old Testament peoples) when I would lose touch with my living Lord. So I thanked God for the three very precious uncluttered months when, because of sick leave, Garth and I had enjoyed sharing and being together, unhindered by ministry demands and commitments. There were times Garth had shared with the children and helped with homework, unheard of in busy days of ministry. Having him at home in the evenings had been pure joy. There was the joy of watching him lead the last Sunday service of his life, just two days before. It was the first time he had led a Sunday service since his sick leave began in November. We had rejoiced together. I thanked the Lord for the special conversation at lunchtime and for the Lord's restoration of me – the completion of a process he had begun some time back. His timing was perfect. I needed to be whole for the demanding future, parenting four children alone. Even as I thanked the Lord a shudder of apprehension and fear swept through me. Yet I knew he had healed me for this.

I thanked God for the few hours Mum and Dad had with Garth and I was just so glad I was there when he died. It could have happened at any time. I was glad to have been with him, even in the agony. I was really glad to have Mum and Dad comfort our children. During the evening's conversation, and in Aneta's prayer, God gave me glimpses of the faith he had planted in the children's hearts that would stand them in good stead in the tough times ahead. I concluded my prayer of thanks, with these words:

> And now Garth is being knit together in the eternal womb of your love. 'It is finished.' His struggle, his pain, his deep unuttered cry are finished and he can nestle at your bosom and absorb the warmth of your love and breathe deep gulps of the fresh wind of the Spirit and drink from clean springs of life-giving water and dance with you in health and great joy.
>
> Tonight I saw the blood shed; the lungs asphyxiated. I experienced all Garth's pain and I knew it was yours also. Only thank you Lord for being with him, loving him and taking him to yourself.
>
> I ache with a deep, deep agony which you Lord know all about. I know you hold me in the palm of your hand. Hold my children also and lead us safely through our grief.

Yes, amazingly, on the night my world broke, I could be glad. I could praise God, experience his overwhelming love, his gift of spiritual communion with Garth and the assurance and peace that came with that. I believe God gave me every consolation that night, out of his heart of love, to equip me for the desolation I was yet to experience.

chapter

two

FROM TRUST, THROUGH TURMOIL, TO TRUST AGAIN

I was not new to receiving God's consolation and all of my experiences in the past had led me to believe he was trustworthy. Over the years God had revealed himself as a God of incredible love and equally incredible power. That awareness had grown through testing times, through the tears, turmoil and triumphs of a very normal life, through marriage, children and ministry.

For as long as I could remember God had been a precious person in my life. I talked freely to him and I asked him confidently about the major decisions I had to make as a young adult. I entered teaching confident of his direction and blessing and loved it. After four years of teaching I met Garth, then a young student for the ministry, doing his summer practical preaching exercise in my home parish. A fast and exhilarating motor bike ride to Dunedin to attend the summer prom concert began our brief courtship. Despite my conservative nature, we were engaged just three months later. I felt I had known Garth for years. Small in stature (we could see eye to eye, both being only 160cm tall) yet with an inner strength that belied his small frame. He cared nothing for appearances but held integrity, honesty and loyalty to be the fabric of relationships. Time and again I watched him cut through people's carefully constructed masks to face the real issues. I could be pushed about by what people thought of me. Nothing and no-one swayed Garth in his quest for truth. Sometimes I squirmed at the bluntness of his honesty. I was much more careful to be 'nice'. Behind his bluntness was a genuine concern and warmth for people. I was sure the Lord was drawing us together, though I initially questioned why he should equip me to teach if I would need a different set of skills as a minister's wife. I was to discover that God wastes nothing. Moses, after being a shepherd for forty years, discovered that all his skills were needed for leading the Israelites through the wilderness. Everything is used in God's economy.

The winter months of 1966 saw Garth braving three-hour, frosty, motorcycle marathons between Dunedin and Alexandra so we could be together. I declined an opportunity to play for the Central Otago Hockey Team at the national tournament, in favour of spending weekends with Garth. The year flew for both of us.

We were in love and felt God's blessing on our lives. We were married in May 1967 amid the glorious autumn colours of my home town in brilliant sunshine, and then it snowed that first honeymoon evening. Seven centimetres of cold crisp whiteness blanketed the silent landscape.

A similar sudden change occurred in our marriage. It went from glowing jubilation and confetti to the crisp cold whiteness of a hospital ward. I fell ill seven weeks after our marriage with a severe kidney infection and there followed weeks of hospitalisation, fear and fervent prayer to our God. We knew little of healing prayer in those days, yet driven by need, Garth and our friends gathered around my bed to pray. Today I am living testimony to God's healing power. It took three long, slow years, but healing came and with it a new awareness of God's love and power.

Amid fear of the unknown and anticipation of God's work, we packed our few belongings in 1969, leaving the student world behind to enter Garth's first parish in Browns, Southland, where Scottish descendants lived in luxurious green rolling sheep country and life moved at a leisurely and considered pace. Traditional patterns persisted long after their usefulness had ended, yet there was a solidarity about Southland; a deep stability coupled with a stubborn tenacity that meant both joy and pain in ministry.

Eight years at Browns taught us a great deal more about our God and about ourselves. We saw the hand of God as our first babies, twin boys, were safely delivered eight weeks premature and each weighing less than one and a half kilograms. My kidneys coped and I bounced back to health. We saw our prayers answered as little Katrina and, later, Aneta joined our family by adoption. We bathed in God's love and the love of parishioners, family and friends.

Yet the parish didn't grow, broken marriages weren't healed, non-Christians still could see no relevance in Jesus. Slowly Garth's dreams of a great work for God died and frustration set in. We began a deep search to discover why our experience of ministry should be so different from the experience of the New Testament Christians as recorded in Acts. We knew God and his love – we lacked his power. We wrestled with a contradiction in our lives. Although God was real, had met us, fed, guided and healed us, we couldn't convey that reality to others.

This concern was still uppermost in our minds when we received a 'call', an invitation, to meet with St Paul's Parish, Feilding to explore the possibility of Garth becoming their minister. We turned to the Lord and in incredible ways he confirmed his calling. I resisted strongly. I like my roots; family and friends. I value the familiar patterns and hate change. But the call was unmistakable and so in October 1977, on Aneta's first birthday, we said our sad goodbyes to the manse at Browns, our first family home, and drove north, leaving behind lovely people, precious memories, good fishing rivers and the fabulous Hollyford country, scene of many special family holidays.

I knew God had called us to Feilding. I immediately loved the little, blue and white, wooden-bungalow manse and its magnificent half-acre garden with tall trees and wilderness corners for energetic seven-year-old boys. I loved the beautiful, light, airy, modern church buildings which were the envy of many a minister. Yet four weeks into our new setting I was so desperately homesick I wanted to curl up and die. I tried to hide my depression. Finally, in tears of frustration, I expressed my feelings to Garth. As he listened and prayed, God lifted my depression. I wasn't troubled again.

In spite of obvious signs of God's presence and power, the awareness grew that we were experiencing but a trickle of what he meant for us and for others. Persistently he drew us in hunger to himself until we let down all our reservations and came to him seeking all he had to offer; open to the Spirit's ministry in us and through us.

It was a real turning point. Changes took place in both of us. Frustrations that used to drive us apart, now drew us together, and to God. Ministry became an exciting, if exhausting, adventure of keeping up with a very active and powerful God. We saw people healed, delivered, saved and growing to maturity in Jesus. The growth was not without pain and fear – the pain of conflict and misunderstanding, and the fear of losing familiar patterns and traditional ways of worshipping. But the pains of a growing church were easier to bear than those of a dying one. We saw God very much alive and active in his body, the Church. Home groups developed and expanded as ministry began to be seen as the task of every Christian. We were busy just keeping abreast with the growth going on in front of our eyes. It was like the rapid growth in a spring garden. It needed shaping, containing, pruning and nourishing. It was a busy season and a whole lot of new learning took place in our understanding of God, his nature and purpose, and his ability to heal and restore broken people.

Life was full, demanding and unpredictable, and with four active children, the days were not long enough. I fell into bed exhausted each night and so did Garth, often much later than I, after attending long meetings or late ministry sessions. I praised God for the vitality he gave me for each day, yet with growing concern I watched Garth's weariness mount. He knew he didn't get enough exercise. That was difficult in a sedentary task. He relaxed with his model trains, a real love since engine-driving days before the call to ministry, and he pottered in a beautiful native corner he had developed at the bottom of our secluded garden. Yet, increasingly, any physical task caused rapid exhaustion, and flus and colds were a recurring feature. It must be admitted that sometimes he enjoyed a cold just because it provided a quiet time to rest and draw pen sketches. Then his silent message to me and others praying for his healing was 'Wait a day or two. Let me enjoy this time before I'm thrown back into business.'

June 1984 saw us both fully occupied in long, full days with a mission to a country parish on the east coast. It was an exhausting week and on returning home Garth promptly developed a cough that persisted despite rest and medication. He became progressively more weary and some days actually stopped work mid-afternoon. I was pleased to see him relaxing a little more, instead of racing from one commitment to the next, but when regular things began to suffer from neglect, and he obviously lacked the energy to attend to them, my concern grew.

A bout of neuralgia necessitated a visit to the doctor and X-rays followed, checking the neuralgia and the persistent cough. Then our doctor ordered tests on the evidence of the X-rays and as a result of those tests our lives took a dramatic turn. The verdict – lung cancer! For a moment my world froze, but the specialist droned on, oblivious of the fact that I was still wrestling with his first sentence. He was talking about the position of the cancer, the impossibility of operating and the need for chemotherapy if Garth wanted a fifteen per cent chance of life. He asked us to decide by Monday and be ready for treatment then, if that was our decision. Monday was three days away!

We drove the twenty kilometres home in silence, buried in our respective thoughts, parked the van and sat on in the garage. Words escaped us. Our feelings were in turmoil. My thoughts raced madly. Why hadn't I suspected? Why hadn't we checked the cough earlier? Why, when Garth had given up smoking years before, had God allowed this? On and on the questions raced. I broke the silence, 'It's not fair! It's just not fair!' I leaned my head on his shoulder, wrapped my arms around him and cried.

In an hour our children would be home from school. What would we tell them? How would they react? In four hours Garth was scheduled to lead a special service of prayer and healing in our church with a guest speaker. Folk who had been praying about Garth's health would want to know the outcome of the tests. When should we tell them? Normally we would have had till Sunday to decide, but with the special service, pretence was not possible. The truth was hard to tell; as hard as it had been to receive.

We agreed that the children needed to know first. In the warm

November evening, as we ate tea under the trees in the garden, Garth told them what was happening and what choices we needed to make. The usual teatime chatter died. The silence was broken by the children's questions.

'Does it mean you are really sick? Do people with cancer die? Are you going to die?'

'But God won't let you.' This from Aneta.

'Do you have to go to hospital? Can you still work and be a minister?' from Katrina, pragmatic and practical.

'If you are off work a long time, will we have to leave the manse, and where will we live?'

What answers could we give them? We had never made promises we couldn't keep or given confident but hollow assurances without any grounds. There are no certainties except the certainty of God's love and our place in him. Together we focused on that and, in prayer, committed ourselves to him in trust and asked his special guidance on the matter of whether to accept chemotherapy as part of his plan for healing.

In the service that evening, one of our precious elders read a brief report Garth had prepared, stating the discovery of the lung cancer and the need for an urgent decision regarding treatment. The warm love of God's people flowed out to meet us. The prayers offered to God that night lifted us right into his wonderful presence and the heaviness and fear of the afternoon fled.

We experienced the strength that comes when God's people keep his commands:

Help carry one another's burdens. (Galatians 6:2)

Pray for one another, so that you will be healed. (James 5:16b)

We believed in a God who heals. We had seen him do it. We had been blessed to be his agents in such healing. He had healed me. It was back in our days at Browns that God had first challenged us to discover that he was still healing today. God had led Garth to pray for two people with cancer.

One prayer had resulted in freedom from pain and that beautiful Christian woman reflected God's own gracious love to many in her last two years. The other person was a much younger woman with a large family. She had been given three months to live. The Lord clearly called Garth to pray for her healing. He argued that he had just brought her finally to an acceptance so necessary for peace. The Lord persisted, giving him the same vision on three successive days. Finally, in fear and trembling, he went to her, against his own instincts, and the Lord responded to his obedience and answered his prayer. The woman lives today; whole by the power of God.

We also firmly believed God heals by various means and medicine was one of his means. We had always been uneasy with the theology of those who insisted that healing only came directly from the hand of God; unable to see his hand in medicine, in human love, in therapy, diet and exercise, in disciplined thought and a healthy lifestyle. Wholeness is a total package from our God who created all things good. Often there are areas that need attention before healing will flow. For example, when illness is obviously aggravated by stress, it is foolish to limit healing to prayer alone. Examination of the lifestyle and adjustments to reduce stress are part of the healing process. We had witnessed instances where resentment, bitterness and unforgiveness were blocking physical healing. Forgiveness and repentance were keys to receiving God's healing in those instances. Only then did prayer have an impact. Only then did God's power flow.

God still heals miraculously and he still heals through many other avenues. Our church contained the whole range of people from those whose God was medicine to those who believed in claiming God's healing as a right; spurning medical assistance as evidence of a lack of trust in God.

We sought the Lord and his will for us and discovered how difficult it is to hear the voice of God above the clamour of our feelings, the noise of our distracted spirits and the whirring of our minds. The one thing we knew for certain was that God was in the business of wholeness in all aspects – spiritual, mental, emotional and physical. We knew beyond doubt that he had been leading Garth, me and his parish into wholeness in wonderful ways.

Wholeness is much more than physical health, though it may include it. Wholeness comes about through renewal and God was renewing us individually and collectively. There had been a powerful realisation that the key to renewal lay in repentance – not an 'I'm sorry, I'll try better' concept, but a life-changing step; dramatic in its release into freedom and growth. We had experienced that deep cleansing; bringing empty selves in total abandonment into the arms of our loving heavenly Father. In that death and resurrection process, which is true repentance and the key to wholeness, we had received from God life in all its fullness.

We had great confidence that if God was concerned to renew us, to guide us, to cleanse us and make us spiritually and emotionally well, then he could also be trusted for physical wholeness. My confidence lay not in hoping for a specific outcome, but in God alone. Even in the confusion of not knowing what specific action to take, I still maintained a deep confidence in him. He was my base line, my rock, and when my feelings spun wildly my spirit still said, 'God is to be trusted.'

Hadn't I discovered that, seventeen years ago, in hospital when I had finally asked for prayer and had put my faith in God to the test? The testing strengthened my faith and proved God's faithfulness. Many times since then we had found God faithful to his Word and to us, his people. A poster expressed well my attitude at this time. Above a stormy scene with a shaft of sunlight penetrating the darkness were the words, '*All I had seen of God taught me to trust him for all I had not seen.*'

chapter

three

REJECTED LOVE

On Tuesday, 27 November at 8.00 a.m. I drove Garth to the hospital to begin the first course of chemotherapy. He looked so alone, so vulnerable, as I left. As a minister, he had seen enough cancer patients to know what he faced.

Feeling cut off and lonely, I drove home. As I set about preparing lunch, the tears streamed down my face and a deep sadness filled my being.

I didn't register the knock at the door. Ann, a dear friend, slipped in, wrapped her arms around me and together we cried; releasing the pent up feelings and sharing our pain. That moment of caring was a special gift. In the months ahead I really treasured the folk who would come and just *be* with me. I discovered the love of God in those who can 'be happy with those who are happy' and 'weep with those who weep' (Romans 12:15).

Later that same Tuesday, another dear parishioner, Irene, brought her daily reading, feeling it was meant to be shared with me. The closing prayer read:

I must have the Saviour with me;
I do not walk alone.

> I must have his presence near me
> And his arms around me thrown.

He had been with me that morning, embodied in Ann, and he was with me now in Irene. I had felt his arms and known his presence.

In the weeks that followed, that love was to embrace us, warm us, encourage and strengthen us. We were amazed at the depth, breadth and height of it. Reflecting the very love of God, people came with monetary gifts, baskets of food, offers of rides to the hospital to keep me company, offers to baby-sit the children and offers to help with the housework. Folk set up a twenty-four hour prayer chain during treatment sessions and joined together in worship to pray for Garth. Letters flowed in from all over the country, some of them very special, and Garth, who had always felt unsure of himself, despite his obvious skills, was completely overwhelmed with the experience of so much love and care.

Sometimes I had to shield him because there were limits to his physical strength. I found it hard to turn away loving people. Some understood and made it easier. Some were offended or just couldn't understand. Some came and prayed with us and we were linked with God and strengthened. Some came and, out of their own need to feel useful, wanted to impose prayer and/or advice whether Garth wished it or not. Those were difficult exhausting visits. I learned that real love is deeply sensitive and listens before it intrudes with preconceived solutions, or exhorts the weary to conjure up faith, to praise ceaselessly, to pray.

I learned the importance of the command, 'Help carry one another's burdens, and in this way you will obey the law of Christ' (Galatians 6:2). The chemotherapy left Garth utterly exhausted. Occasionally depression descended upon him. Sometimes he would wake from a nightmare in a cold sweat. At such times it was my task and gift to carry him in prayer; to lift him in his weakness to the Lord, just as he, when strong in the past, had so often stood alongside the weak and interceded for them. There is a need for the Church today to be burden bearers; to lift the weak, the sorrowing and the crushed in spirit into Christ's presence; to stand alongside, in a quality of commitment akin to that of Christ. As Jesus does not condemn weakness (as Romans 8 would suggest), neither should we.

Life changed dramatically for us with treatments every three weeks, and recuperation periods between, when Garth was nauseated and tired. He was relieved of all parish responsibilities. There were huge adjustments for him to make. From a position of leadership he now had to trust the parishioners to respond to all the needs and tasks within the church. Likening the church to a ship, he said, 'I feel as if I hold the rudder in my hands but have been cut off from the ship itself. I feel so useless. I long to steer the ship again.' The church leaders felt abandoned in the ship without the rudder. It was a crisis time. But within an amazingly short period, they took control with commitment and ability, steering a course that gladdened Garth's heart.

Meals had to be adjusted as nausea increased and tastes changed. Garth developed a real desire for a cold beer – he who had seldom consumed alcohol in any form. I remember upsetting a dear Salvation Army friend, quite unwittingly, when she enquired about his health. I replied that he was existing on a diet of bean salad, chicken nibbles and beer. I think the respect she had for Garth took a tumble that day.

The children adjusted to having Garth at home. For a while they walked around him like a piece of furniture, still half expecting him to be preoccupied with business. With time they grew to enjoy leisurely sharing and assistance with homework, and model making.

One of the side effects of chemotherapy, the total loss of all hair, provided both anxiety and moments of humour. It has been said that a woman's hair is her crowning glory. I think that applies equally to men. Losing one's hair gradually is difficult enough, but to lose it all practically overnight is humiliating and we found that the children struggled with it as much as Garth. When Garth was deciding whether he would live with baldness or wear a wig, he found the decision made for him when the girls stated that they would be embarrassed to go down the street with him if he were bald. Their embarrassment was actually greater than Garth's. Occasionally Garth's wicked sense of humour got the better of him. He would startle a friend who didn't know he was wearing a wig by simply lifting it off, delighting in their shocked reaction.

Life revolved around Garth's fluctuating health. Treatment times were tough and for several days afterwards he was quite ill. At those times we appreciated the prayerful support of parish and family.

On one occasion, I was waiting at the hospital while Garth underwent tests. I had known moments of peace since November but my swirling emotions often clouded my spiritual perception that God was in control. On this occasion I was tired and dispirited from nights of broken sleep. Aimlessly, I flicked through the outdated magazines strewn on the coffee table. Nothing took my fancy. I was anxious about Garth and the articles seemed trivial. My eyes swept about the clinical room with its white plaster walls. Breaking the bleakness were five scenes from a New Zealand calendar, sellotaped to the wall by a sensitive staff member. As I drank in those scenes I suddenly felt as if I were in each of them. In the first, a Fiordland mountain scene, I was climbing a rocky cliff and about to round a point. Ahead was a deep river valley shrouded in mist. In the second, I was ascending the steep face of a cliff with the ocean pounding below.

In the third, I was tumbling through rapids in a fast flowing southern river and, in the fourth, I was precariously edging my way across a wire rope bridge above a deep, bush-clad gully and a roaring, icy river. The panic, submerged in my subconscious for days, surfaced forcefully. My spirit cried out to the Lord, 'Where are you right now in each of those scenes?' I focused on the first calendar scene again. This time I knew the Lord was in the mist just around the corner calling me to come. In the ocean scene, he was just below me on the cliff track, encouraging me to continue to climb. In the river scene, he was standing waist deep in the freezing river beckoning me to trust him to catch me, and on the wire bridge he was backing across just ahead of me, his eyes on me all the time, encouraging me to continue towards him.

Suddenly a deep, deep peace flooded my whole being. I knew that the Lord had spoken through those scenes to still the storm raging in my emotions, just as long ago he had spoken to still the wind and waves and they had obeyed. My emotions responded to his voice and quietened. That incredible peace that Jesus speaks of in John 14:27, stayed with me right through the remaining months of Garth's illness. It was a peace that didn't mean the absence of pain or suffering or struggle, but a deep peace that under-girded it all; a solid base of hope and trust. It was that solid base of peace that enabled me, in the face of Garth's illness and gloomy medical prognosis, to write as the concluding sentence in our 1984 Christmas newsletter to friends:

> We don't know what 1985 will hold but we do know who holds 1985. That for us is peace and joy.

The peace persisted. So too did Garth's coughing; the cause of my broken sleep. It intensified, causing real discomfort and eventually resulting in broken ribs. I found myself tensing with him as he doubled up to cough. Yet I couldn't carry his pain. In fact, in many ways, I was feeling very apart from Garth and very helpless. Always, in ministry, we had carried things together. We had shared and prayed, wept and laughed together. But the illness was different. I felt alone, abandoned in waiting rooms at the hospital, on the sideline at home, watching his pain and his inner spiritual and emotional struggle. The deeper his struggle the greater the distance grew between us.

The whole problem of isolation – longing to enter and carry some of his agony – came to a head in January. We abandoned a long-planned trip to visit my family in the South Island and chose instead a restful holiday at a nearby beach. Garth felt inadequate in his inability to pack the van. My loading heavy cases and boxes of supplies simply compounded the problem. He withdrew in humiliation and rejected my love.

At the holiday house the pain intensified and the coughing spasms increased. He was physically exhausted, yet unable to rest because every twenty minutes brought another ten minute coughing bout. There was little relief day or night. I wanted so much to hold him and absorb the pain. He didn't want to be touched, preferring to struggle alone.

At dawn I walked the beach alone with an ache so deep I thought it would tear me apart. But as well as the ache I experienced deep anger. Where did it spring from? I walked and walked, feeling the sand through

Shattered and Restored

my toes, the wind in my face. Then I sat on a log and watched the ceaseless lapping of the waves and listened to the mournful cries of the gulls. I wrote of my pain to the Lord:

> I can't enter his pain.
> At its worst he is most alone.
> A wall I can't penetrate;
> Off which my love bounces back to me
> And I become hurt and angry.
> I sit with him and he does not acknowledge me.
> I go from him and he seems not to care.
> His world stops with him
> And my aching love has nowhere to go.
> It cannot be received
> And certainly can't be returned in a response
> That warms and accepts me.
> There is my anger! I see its cause now.
> My human love demands a response.
> It is wounded when it hits a wall
> And is tossed back – an unopened gift.
>
> I see your pain now, Lord,
> As your gift was rejected, trampled on.
> Hosea speaks of your love
> And the people's rejection of it.
> You went on loving.
> It's your nature to love,
> But I sense it hurt you, too,
> Each time it was rejected.
> I am wounded for two reasons:
> I can't help when he needs it most – Love lies unopened;
> I am thwarted in my need to give
> And in my need to receive a response.

How vastly different is your unconditional love
From my human love flowing out of my own needs
And expecting fulfilment.
Lord, I need to be filled with your kind of love.
Only then will I not grow angry
And become swallowed up in loneliness and self.

I've tasted the bitter flavour of rejected love
That was your cross;
That was part of your pain.
And you forgave and went on loving;
Embracing the cross.
It is your very nature to love.

I pondered Jesus' ability to embrace pain and to withstand rejection from those he loved so deeply.

All my life I had tried to avoid pain. It seems a natural human reaction. When one of my children skins a knee, they come running to me, yet withdraw it from me, even as I try to cleanse it. In deep emotional pain we also withdraw and say, 'Don't touch.' In doing so we shut out the love and healing we need. Garth did that, pushing away my love. Later I would do the same to Jesus, crying out to him, yet withdrawing, saying in effect, 'Don't touch. It hurts too much.' So I would miss his presence and be deaf to his words.

In August 1984, before Garth's illness, I had accepted an invitation to act as a spiritual director at a Christian retreat. Whilst I was there several situations led to my growing awareness that the fullness of life is only experienced when we are prepared to embrace the pain of life as well as the joy. To run away from risks and pain is to become stifled and imprisoned, and ultimately to die spiritually. For the first time in my life, I think, I grasped that pain and joy are inseparable.

In prayer, dwelling on the crucifixion, I experienced Mary's pain for Jesus, and wrote of it:

Shattered and Restored

    Pain. Ugliness.
        Scarred legs. Bleeding hearts.
            Arms reaching in agony and emptiness.
A silent cry tears at the gut.
        A wail of anguish sends jagged sound waves
            through the still air.
Pain is to be avoided at all costs,
Or is it?
I fear it. I avoid it.
I move in ever restricted places,
Safe, but imprisoned.
        No room to move, to explore,
            To stretch, to risk,
                To plunge in.
No scope to touch life,
      Feel its pulse,
           Dance to its music
                Or embrace its colour.
Life is pain and joy,
      Dark and light,
           Death and life.
From the dead seed life bursts forth.
        Through pain joy shines.
            The shadows are created by the light.
To avoid pain is to be nothing,
      To do nothing,
           To see and feel and touch nothing,
                To be imprisoned.
I identify with the empty cross.
      Feeling its joy and freedom,
            its life and victory.
But it embraced pain in all its agony.
Held tight to pain,
      Accepted its scars,

>   Welcomed the broken heart,
>   Absorbed it.
> And waited, and waited…
> In death victory came, the light shone,
>   The Son rose, life burst forth.
>   Three days of pain,
>   An eternity of joy.
> Now I see. I embrace life, step into it.
> And when it pains me and agony is its lot
> I will go to the cross.
> There to have the pain absorbed;
>   To rise victorious again,
>   Free to enter all of life
>   With HIM.

I had written that in August, before Garth's illness. I had pronounced my willingness to experience all of life. Then, at the beach house, when the reality of that pain hit as my love was spurned, I discovered my reluctance to embrace the cross. I turned away from it, even as Garth in his pain turned away from me. I was not good at coping with pain; not good at loving as Jesus did, in spite of rejection. I sat on the water-worn log at the beach that morning struggling with pregnant love that could not be delivered and as the sun rose and cast a golden glow across the lapping waters, a deep admiration for Jesus also rose within me and he touched my wounded spirit with his unquenchable love.

chapter

four

HE SETS THE CAPTIVES FREE

Three months later the rejection was final. My love would be forever unopened. Garth was dead. In the night my world had exploded. With the light of day, the cold, hard fact of Garth's death began to seep through my being into the marrow of my bones. My stomach churned and my heart pounded a message at my ribcage: '*He's dead. He's dead.*' Yet, shock enabled me to function. I, who had so often told Garth that I would never manage without him, was at that moment managing in ways that astounded me.

I was still numb. I had not slept, yet I didn't register my own weariness. I was upheld by the knowledge that Garth was finally free from his struggle and with Jesus. The gift that God had given me in the spiritual presence of Garth, our sharing and final goodbyes, still warmed my heart. I truly believed that God held 1985.

The day passed in busyness as one caller after another came, brought gifts, expressed sympathy, cried, hugged, shared precious memories, drank cups of tea, and left. Mum busied herself with meals and dishes all day. I was barely aware of the hum of activity from the church next door where the seminar, which Garth should have introduced and which Mum and I had planned to attend, got under way. They were speaking about healing.

I was living a death. Not a moment passed when I did not think about Garth.

By mid-evening, when all the children were back in bed and the house was quiet, I was aware that my mind was trapped, caught up in the memories of the night before. They flooded back as I lived and relived Garth's last moments. I knew I would never sleep like that, and I felt physically sick and fearful. I walked restlessly through the house, trying to shake the memories off. They persisted.

The lights were still on in the church. Bill and Delores had been ministering all day to a parish in grief, speaking of the healing power of Jesus. I needed that healing power desperately. So, at 10.00 p.m., I slipped over to the church, just as they were leaving. I went to speak. Only tears came. Delores' embrace drew out all the dammed up tears until I was able to tell her of my need.

They came home, and in gentle love and the power of the Lord, they prayed with me in the bathroom. As they anointed me and the room with oil, they asked the Lord to heal the memories, to cleanse the room and to heal my wounded spirit.

As Bill and Delores prayed, they pictured Jesus standing in the corner of the room picking Garth up, just as I had experienced the previous night. As they prayed, the fear dissipated. I haven't been troubled by that scene since then. I can remember and see it, but the horror and fear have gone. I slept soundly from 11.00 p.m. till 5.00 a.m.

I'm not usually a very observant person, yet I seemed finely tuned to my children's feelings in the days immediately following Garth's death.

I watched Ian two days after his Dad's death and I saw fear and deep pain in his eyes. He looked like a wounded animal. I discovered that he was struggling deeply, as I had, with replays of Garth's death, which he had witnessed. He couldn't sleep and kept trying to switch his mind to other things. But every time he shut his eyes, he was back in the grip of fear. I prayed with him and led him through the memory of Tuesday. God gave him the most beautiful picture of Jesus taking Garth up a wide staircase into heaven. He saw him well and whole, in his working clothes (the way he best liked to see him) speaking, breathing, sharing with Jesus.

It was a precious gift and he slept in peace.

Jim faced the same problem the following night, with the additional fear of always, in his nightmare, seeing Satan standing in the doorway, laughing. It was many months before I dared share with anyone my own experience of the demonic nature of Garth's death. Right now, I was not going to tell Jim his nightmare reflected my own experience. I just called on the Lord to heal and restore Jim's memories. As he described what he saw in prayer, he added, 'Jesus has picked Dad up. The room has filled with light. Satan has fled down the passage and out the door.' The whole scene was cleansed for him. The light from heaven had touched the empty shell of his Dad on the floor and it had simply melted away, leaving a clean scene and a vivid awareness of his living Dad with Jesus in heaven.

Katrina had not seen Garth die, and for that, I was deeply grateful. No child needs that kind of trauma. I recalled Rob Cameron saying, at some stage on Tuesday, that the children would need help as a result of all they had seen. I didn't know what help he had in mind, if anything, but God was definitely able. His help was sufficient.

I thought Aneta was okay. She had been awake on Tuesday and aware of Garth's death when I went to tell her, but I couldn't recall seeing her in the hallway earlier. She hadn't spoken of his death. But on Friday morning I watched her wrap her little arms around her Daddy's chair and cuddle it in a silent, hungry gesture, as if desperately trying to get near him. Always before she had got close to him; spent hours with him in his illness, stroking him, sitting on his lap. How she missed his touch and cuddles. My heart ached for her emptiness. As I tucked her into bed that night, I listened as she spoke of what she had seen. The pictures wouldn't go away. She was scared and sad. She had seen it all.

I wasn't sure if she could handle the inner healing prayer. 'O, Lord,' I prayed silently, 'she's so little, but she needs your healing. Please help her.' Like the disciple I prayed, 'Lord, I believe. Help my unbelief.'

I took Aneta back deliberately into that bathroom scene in her mind, and made her picture it clearly. Then I asked her to picture Jesus there. I waited a few moments in silence, then asked, 'Is Jesus standing in the bathroom?'

She replied, 'Oh, no! He's kneeling and stroking Daddy's head.'

I asked her to watch what Jesus did. With her little head snuggled in her pillow and her eyes shut, she told me that he had picked Daddy up and they were going up a very wide, beautiful, shiny staircase. I was struck by the similarity with the boys' prayer images, and testing her, I asked if Jesus was carrying Daddy. She said, 'Oh, no! He's walking. He's strong, he's well and they're talking.' They came to the top where it was flat, and she continued, 'Daddy's picking a red rose and giving it to Jesus and now Jesus is showing him around heaven and it's absolutely beautiful. The sun's shining. There is a lovely rainbow.' All this she saw so clearly. It was an absolute joy.

I could have stopped there, but I knew that wasn't enough. I had to take her back to discover again, as I had with the boys, what was left on the bathroom floor.

She said, 'Daddy's body is there, and all the blood.' I asked her if the light that she saw in heaven could reach down into the bathroom. She said, 'Oh, yes! It's just pouring down, and the body has all melted away, and the floor is clean and shiny, like when it's polished.' And she gave a big smile. I could see the relief flood right through her body. She just lay there in deep joy, and dropped off to sleep. That scene hasn't bothered her since and I doubt it ever will. I'm just so grateful to God for his healing.

One would think that never again could I doubt the power or love of God who could minister so amazingly. Yet, in the next year, I was to doubt that love, challenge his power, question his very existence. I would be unable to pray, unable to find this very God who had heard and answered my prayers this night. I would be trapped in a pit of despair, distrust and disillusionment. All I would have left of my relationship with Jesus would be memories of past encounters. Finally, the truth would win through and realities, such as my children's healing, which remained complete, would have their say, but not till many months of darkness and spiritual struggle had passed.

chapter

five

HE COMFORTS ALL WHO MOURN

Life doesn't stop while we reassemble the broken pieces. It marches right on. Death is an end and a beginning. A life has ended, a grief begun, and the funeral often marks this turning point. We had funeral arrangements to make. The only one who was familiar with the practical aspects of funerals wasn't here; it was his funeral. I was out of my depth. The children had talked a little about his funeral the night he died. So together we chose format, songs, minister, etc. Unanimously, the children rejected cremation and expressed their desire to go to the cemetery.

Garth had firmly believed that children needed to be involved, not shielded from reality. They ought to be allowed to experience the loss and grieve openly. Healing, he believed, was found in facing reality and working through it. He had never discussed this with the children. Instinctively, they knew what was right for them. They also wanted to see his body because they had unfinished business with him and the Lord. We went together. Each prayed in turn, asking Jesus to pass their love on to their Dad. They said the things that there had been no opportunity to say. For them, it was a healing time. For them, there would be no unfinished business to haunt their future.

The children found support with their friends in the days immediately after Garth's death. On the day of the funeral, Jim's friend, Andrew, wanted to come. 'Where should he sit?' Jim asked. I replied, 'Beside you.' Jim said, 'But I thought only the family sat in the front pew.' It is my view that love wins over convention every time. If he needed his friend with him, then that's where Andrew should be. So it was that we filed into church and took up the whole front row; both Garth's parents and mine with me, and my children each with a special friend for support. Those friends were a blessing to my children in the days following. They helped them in their pain just by being there and by being so normal; playing cricket, monopoly, romping and yarning.

Garth had detested eulogies, believing a funeral should glorify God, not man. We focused on God. The glory of the Lord filled the church. With strength and conviction we sang *Our God Reigns* – Garth's favourite proclamation of God's sovereignty.

As a special gift that only God could have arranged, a beautiful young singer, and loved member of our song group for several years before moving away, was in Feilding the day of Garth's death and agreed to sing at his funeral. Sue's clear, strong voice filled the church with the poignant words of *Be Still My Soul*. Her radiant smile and faith in God ministered in a very special way to the packed church, touching people in the depth of their spirits and affirming God as Lord; the one who, 'through every change, faithful will remain.' For the next few weeks, I often heard Katrina singing that hymn around the house, letting the words minister to her wounded spirit; letting her God still the restless storm in her soul.

All of us were restless, nerve ends exposed and raw, experiencing the physical pain of grief in all its fullness. Aneta couldn't eat. Her stomach tied itself in knots. Mine did too. The tension felt the same as fear, as before a public performance. It was some time before I recognised that the feeling was not in fact fear but grief, and the recognition brought relief, as I read C. S. Lewis:

> No one ever told me that grief felt so like fear, I'm not afraid but the sensation is like being afraid, the same fluttering in the stomach, the same restlessness, the yawning. I keep on swallowing.[1]

The feeling would build up to an unbearable level and then the tears would flow, initially several times a day, and then every few days. The shower proved a good place to cry. A friend called one morning as I was sobbing my way through a shower. I called out, 'I'll see you in a minute when I'm dry.' She called back, with warm compassion, 'Do you ever think you will get dry that way?'

The morning, just when the children had all left the house and the awful silence and emptiness descended upon me, was a time of deep grief and frequent tears. Also, late at night, when I slipped across in the dark to lock up the church, I was acutely aware of the loss of Garth. The dark and silent study, every object and book speaking of his life and work stopped in its tracks. The empty church seemed to echo his name in the silence. Many a night the build up of tension and grief found release in tears in the quiet sanctuary of the church, the dim lights picking out the outline of the empty cross, echoing the emptiness in my heart.

Yet the tears were healing. They brought release. They were necessary. How important it is to be real in ourselves and with God. I fear for those forced by shallow doctrine to praise the Lord anyway and to be joyful in all situations. Such falsehood breeds deep trouble and I find no Scripture to support pretence with God at any point. He knew my heart was broken. What good would it do to pretend it wasn't? I needed to present him with the broken pieces, that he might mend them with my cooperation. A quick glance through the Psalms will show how honest David and others were with God about their condition. Jesus on the cross, feeling utterly isolated, did not pretend he was enjoying the suffering. Instead he cried, 'My God, why did you abandon me?' That is what it felt like to him and he told God so.

I had learned in the past that my prayers bounced off the ceiling when I pretended with God; when I hid the reality I felt within. In grief, when emotions ran strong, I told God about it. I shared it all with him. I found release in writing to Jesus in my prayer diary. With release, came the ability to hear his Word to me. Until release came there was such a storm raging within me that it was quite impossible to hear his voice.

One such storm was the fear of being cut off from a wide circle of friends Garth and I had developed within the Presbyterian ministry. Because of the nature of our work, many of my friends were ministers and their wives. I was deeply afraid that, as I walked new paths and moved out of that central place in church life, there would be no point of contact with those people. Without Garth, or a common task, I feared we would grow apart. Loneliness gripped me, almost a sense of panic, and it drowned out the assurances God was offering – that he knew my need and would meet it. Several of these friends, by their constant love, regular letters, and gifts, finally quietened my fears and I recognised the gift God had given me in their friendship.

The reality of death takes time to register and even then, it breaks like waves on the shore, slips away and then breaks again, unexpectedly.

Ian was playing his cornet with the local brass band one evening about a week after Garth's death. Suddenly, in the middle of a tune, the realisation broke upon him that he would never see his Dad again; never enjoy the model trains with him, or help build tree huts. Never would they pore over stamps together or laugh at favourite TV programmes. He choked inside and couldn't play another note.

Katrina felt a different loss. She had loved responding to her Dad's invitation, 'What shall we sing in church on Sunday?' She had helped him choose the songs and, sometimes, with her sweet true voice, helped lead them. She missed the involvement.

Aneta missed his touch. Each day, some new loss swept over us, knocking us off balance again.

Good Friday dawned clear and sunny. We drove to a beautiful bush reserve where the boys were to join one hundred youngsters at a Christian camp. We were early. I wandered through the native bush, pausing at the outdoor chapel – a rough cross erected by tall totara trees. A shaft of light beamed down upon it through the canopy of leaves. The bush was full of life and growth and rich decaying death, bringing in turn new life – all in harmony. The bellbirds and tuis sang triumphantly of freedom. The trees were a masterpiece from God's own hand. I felt his presence, experienced the enormity of his sacrifice, his huge love and open arms.

With the boys settled, the girls and I picnicked in the sun, tall trees at our backs. The girls ran off to swing on a tree and I lay on my back, cushioned in the soft grass, bathing in the warmth. I felt so glad to experience it all. Then I cried because I couldn't share it with Garth. Yet I felt he knew it all and after the tears the joy persisted in all its richness. I felt like a seed emerging from its dark shell. I heard the promise, 'Those who sow in tears will reap with songs of joy' (Psalm 126:5 NIV). Truly, I experienced the death and resurrection of Easter as never before.

Suddenly, the girls' laughter died away. All was silent. I sat up to see where they were. Aneta called out in obvious relief, 'Oh, it's all right. I thought you were dead.'

Reflecting on her statement, I realised the level of her insecurity. If one parent could suddenly drop out of her world, what was to guarantee it couldn't happen to the other as well. Her childlike trust had been shattered. I gave her a cuddle, assured her I was very much alive, and she bounded off to play.

That Good Friday was a beautiful day. God's creation praised him, and I could, too. I drove back to Feilding warm in heart, looking forward to tea with a friend. She had realised the girls and I would be alone and she didn't want that for us so soon after Garth's death. Unbeknown to me, she had invited a few couples I knew, to share the meal. A wave of panic swept over me when I saw them all. Suddenly, I couldn't cope. I was aware of the couples, all cheerfully chatting together. I felt utterly bereft. They all had husbands. I was single. I struggled through half my meal, choking on each mouthful, before I slipped to the bathroom, burst into tears, and let the pent-up feelings pour out. Washed and composed again, I rejoined those friends, but the evening was difficult. I just wanted to run away and hide. I felt naked in my singleness and very vulnerable.

At unexpected times, the loneliness engulfed me. I felt cut in half. Garth was present in my thoughts all the time. I seemed to be lost. I didn't know who I was any more. I had been Elsa, Garth's wife, minister's wife. Who was I now? Elsa, solo parent, widow.

We all had strong reactions to the word 'widow'. The children hated it. It conjured up mental pictures of little old ladies, frail and living alone. Ironically, Katrina, at that time, had the major part in the school's drama presentation, as 'Widow Twanky'. In this role she pleaded with the cruel landlord not to throw her out as she 'had nowhere to go'. I did not face cruel church officers, intent on throwing me out; quite the reverse. But we did have to find somewhere to go, and I jokingly suggested Katrina enact it before the congregation. She could be Widow Twanky and I could be 'Widow Cranky', which was how I felt.

The stigma attached to solo parents in New Zealand left me joyless about accepting that label, and the humiliation of having to join the Social Welfare system by applying for a widows' benefit, did nothing positive for my crushed self-worth. Sometimes I could laugh at the situation; more often I wanted to cry.

Fear of the future filled me. Garth and I had ministered to enough single parents and their children to know the incompleteness of a broken family and the devastating effect that has on all involved. Wholeness seemed an impossible dream in those circumstances, and ministry appeared only to shore them up for a while.

In my fear, I cried out to God, voicing my deep concerns to him in a time alone in the church:

> I feel alone and hurting, unclean, somehow leprous, and definitely not whole. I am grieved and angry with you because you are in the business of wholeness – whole people, whole marriages, families and churches, communities. You had been enriching our marriage, bringing a beautiful wholeness, and suddenly it's all been snatched away and I feel cut in half and aching to be whole.

Ringing in my mind was an old hymn:

> Take my cup, Lord. I lift it up, Lord.
> Come and quench this thirsting of my soul.
> Bread of Heaven, feed me till I want no more.
> Take my cup, fill it up, and make me whole.

I sang the words through my pain to Jesus and, as I sang, I felt my cup, like his, was a bitter one. In the singing, I realised I had to lift it up, not cling to it in self-pity. I had to surrender it to the Lord, lift it to him, to be filled with the blood of the New Covenant and claim the promise found in Isaiah 54. I opened the church Bible on the communion table and read aloud in the light which shone from behind the empty cross:

> Do not be afraid
> You will forget your desperate loneliness as a widow.
> Your Creator will be like a husband to you –
> The Lord Almighty is his name.
> 'I will show you my love forever.'
> So says the Lord who saves you.
> 'My love for you will never end;
> I will keep forever my *promise of peace*.'
> So says the Lord who *loves* you.
> (Isaiah 54:4–10 italics mine)

In the dimly lit and silent church, I knew the Lord had heard my heart-cry, had listened to my angry accusations, had hung and died for me. It was ugly. Awful. I knew that if he went through all that for me, he was not about to abandon me now. A deep awareness grew in me that we were a whole family. With God as my husband, and father to my children, we could be whole. I did not have to make decisions alone. I could make them in consultation with God. It was still possible to stay warm and glowing in the radiance of his love.

I left the church comforted; a deep peace in my spirit, the assurance that God cared and that I was not alone. In the eyes of the world I was single. With the eyes of my spirit, I now saw it differently.

Oh, to be able to report that we lived happily ever after. Only fairy tales end that way, and everyone knows they are not true. I had moments of intense aching for loving human embrace. Garth had always made me feel beautiful and feminine. Now I felt about as feminine as a block of concrete. Tinges of jealousy surfaced as I saw the beauty in Katrina, and knew that ahead of her, possibly, lay romance and marriage.

I ached for what I had lost. Garth's brother and sister-in-law came to stay a few days with us. They have a beautiful marriage, which gladdens my heart, yet their very closeness put the spot light on my loneliness and loss. At such times, I struggled for a middle course between denial of what was happening in me and the danger of wallowing in self-pity. I needed to face reality, acknowledge the pain, and crawl into God's arms for his healing touch, then positively praise him for the healthy marriages I saw around me; signs of his love and grace.

This middle course was not easy to maintain. I recall a day I battled with loneliness and how to deal with it positively, in ways that brought healing, and not destruction. It was a holiday, two months after Garth's death, and we were all feeling in need of a break. We packed a picnic lunch and drove to Wanganui, a nearby city with beautiful parks. We had been there on many occasions in the past. It held fond memories for all of us. Perhaps that's what drew us back. Yet, at the playground, the children bounded out of the car, scrambled all over the play equipment, and I was left standing alone.

At the water tower, the children raced ahead up 169 steps at a speed far in excess of my ability. I walked alone, where once Garth would have walked beside me. Finally, at the beautiful lake, as the children raced off along the tree-lined track like frisky puppies revelling in the space and warm sunshine, tears welled up inside me and loneliness engulfed me.

The children were reacting as they always did. Only, in the past, Garth had walked with me and we had talked, enjoyed the scenery together and shared lunch, while the children scrambled up banks or tree trunks. Now I walked alone. I wanted to run from that place, to escape the pain. I knew that would be foolish. I loved this place. We had precious memories of times together here. Blotting it out would solve nothing. I very nearly fell into the grip of self-pity. Somehow, by God's grace, I stopped short of that. Instead, I told God how lonely and lost I felt; how much I was missing my best friend's company. I cried. Then deliberately, I recalled the good times, thanked the Lord for them, and went on to share the walk around the lake with Jesus, thanking him for its beauty; seeing his creativity in colourful autumn leaves, in the swans and the wild ducks.

It was a difficult, painful day. Yet through it, God met me and taught me a lot about the right and wrong ways to handle grief. The memory of that day came back to me on other occasions when I felt sorry for myself. It helped me focus on the positive and to thank God for the good things.

In theory, I knew all the stages of grief. I had read all about them and sought to help others work through their grief. The theory makes good sense. The reality is difficult. I recognised the anger when it surfaced, as one of the stages of grief, but knowing it was normal did not, in any way, diminish its intensity. My anger put distance between me and my Lord. From such isolation one day I wrote to the Lord:

Dear Jesus,

I ache to hear from you. You said you would be a husband to the widow. Well, husbands talk and I haven't heard from you for three weeks. I ache for a letter from you. Write soon. I need to hear from you. I've said so much to you and written pages these last three weeks. Is my mail stacked unopened in your letterbox? Have you gone on holiday? Am I talking to an answer phone? I don't know when, if ever; you will get to replying. Please talk to me now. Please tell me what is on your heart!

Then with pen in hand I chose an idea first suggested by Matthew and Denis Lynn, Jesuit priests, as one way of listening to God. They suggested writing a letter in reply, as from the Lord, sensing what he wanted to say.

I prayed, 'Jesus speak to me,' and I began to write, hesitantly at first. Then suddenly, I was hearing the Lord's words and simply writing what he spoke to me:

Dear Elsa,

I'm hurting. I've loved you in a thousand ways these three weeks. I've kept the path light, watched all night over you and embraced your children. But there's a barrier between us and you are suspicious of me.

> You are holding me responsible for Garth's death and asking me to explain myself and, while you've been waving the verdict 'guilty' in my face, you've missed all the tears I've shed and the pain in my heart for you.

My pen dropped to the floor and I cried as I recognised the agony of Jesus' love and my rejection of it. It brought back memories of Garth rejecting my love in his pain filled days in January and I saw Jesus' grief in a whole new way. My anger dissolved in the light of his great love.

But my anger had not only been directed towards the Lord. It was also directed towards Garth. On one occasion, I sought the seclusion of our native corner in the garden to deal with this tension. Suddenly, the anger gripped me and, with explosive force, I let fly a barrage of frustration towards Garth, 'Why did you have to go and die now? How dare you cop out of the responsibilities of raising our four children. Why have you left it all to me? Why didn't you give up smoking when God first told you to? Do you see where your resistance has landed the rest of us? How could you be so selfish?' I frightened myself with the strength of my anger. And still it came. Finally, when it was finished, I went on in the quietness of that secluded corner to forgive Garth for his contribution to our present brokenness and to seek God's forgiveness for my contribution and for my anger. I felt the Lord's cleansing. I felt the restoration between Garth and me; the unity that comes through repentance and forgiveness. I was a little bit further along the thorny pathway of grief; a little bit more whole.

chapter

six

MY WILL, NOT YOURS, BE DONE

I've sat, pen poised above paper, on numerous fruitless occasions, struggling to assemble this chapter in some order. Unfortunately the months of grief I now try to write about were lived in total chaos. The notes in my diary swing from despair to hope then back to despair; from anger to peaceful submission then back to confused anger again. One day I wrote of my love for Jesus and the security I felt in him. The next day I wrote of crippling fear and alienation.

How could I be so muddled and inconsistent and, more to the point, how can I now present that time in some logical sequence? Perhaps I can't, because in the midst of deep grief, orderly progress is an empty dream. The reality is like a butterfly's flight: erratic, soaring upward to catch the sun, plummeting down to new depths, resting a while in a sheltered spot, then, with tender wings, battling the wind again to meet life's demands.

One of the Oxford Dictionary's definitions of 'grief' is: 'Deep sorrow caused by loss'. One can grieve for lost belongings, lost youthfulness, lost eyesight in old age, lost dreams, lost opportunities. Garth's death precipitated an avalanche of losses. In addition to losing Garth, I lost my identity, my trust in God's unfailing goodness and love, my confidence,

Shattered and Restored

my self-worth, my sense of security, my direction and purpose in life, my familiar surroundings and work.

In the past on hiking expeditions, I've been surrounded by tall native bush, yet totally unafraid because I've known the way out. That same sweet-smelling, sheltered canopy of trees could be a source of fear had I lost my sense of direction. The circular movement of the writing in my diary shows I was lost, searching for a way out of the dark smothering canopy of grief. I had no sense of direction.

I had no sense of self either. 'Who am I, God?' was a question often on my heart. People knew me as 'the minister's wife, Garth's wife'. 'Who am I now? Did people want to know me before just because of my position? Will they still want to know me – for myself?' There was within me an incredible desire to be known. Garth had always known me. Without a word spoken he understood. Now I had to keep bringing people up-to-date and I longed for one who just *knew me*. I found my longing reflected in the heart of God in Hosea:

> What I want from you is plain and clear: I want your constant love ...
> I would rather have my people *know me* than burn offerings to me.
> (Hosea 6:5, 6 italics mine)

He knew. He understood. His longing was the same. He knew me. And he desires to be known by us. He wants to share a deep communion and a constant love with us.

Numerous little incidents highlighted my identity crisis. I had always spoken of *our* children, *our* van.

Suddenly it was *my* van, and they were *my* children and I choked over that little pronoun. I remember wrapping Katrina's birthday present, happily anticipating her pleasure. I filled in the card with joy and signed it, 'With love from Mum'. Fullstop. The reality hit with unexpected force. It had always been 'Mum and Dad' before. We belonged together. The greeting felt as strangely incomplete as I did.

A dear friend of Garth's called one day. It was a special time. I greatly valued his friendship. Yet when he left, a gnawing ache filled me. Colin

My Will, Not Yours, Be Done

was missing Garth. So was I and I was no substitute for his friend.

In the early days of grief I struggled with folk who chattered non-stop, deliberately avoiding any mention of Garth. It was as if they wanted to chop off seventeen years of my life; to pretend those years never existed. I wanted to remember, to talk of him, to print firmly in my memory those precious years, to savour every rich moment, lest I lose them as well as him. The feeling of singleness dogged me often. I shared my feelings with Jesus:

Lord,

A deep ache fills me when I watch couples. I feel cheated, abandoned – the love you brought us into suddenly whipped away.

I don't like the new labels with which people identify me: widow, solo mother, beneficiary. I feel less of a human being now. Lord, I want to go unlabelled, accepted for who I am. Yet who am I? I don't know any more.

I heard the Lord's response:

Elsa,

I know who you are. I called you by name and you belong to me. I delight in you. I need no labels to relate to you. I know you intimately and am grieving for you. I feel your pain. I've heard your anger. Come aside with me. Be still with me. See the love I have for you. Let the anger flow out till all the doubts, questions and fears are dissolved. Receive my love, rich and true and tender.

The turning point came on that occasion when, in the church one evening, the Lord's words spoke to me from Isaiah 54. It was the beginning of the restoration of my identity and hope for wholeness in the future. I discovered what the Word of God has always said – that my identity is found in God alone. The world may label me this or that. It may be good or bad. The labels change – teenager, student, teacher, wife, mother, widow – but one label never changes. It is the label that declares I am a child of God, a daughter of the King. I needed to re-establish my identity in that which lasts forever.

Closely allied to identity is a sense of self-worth. I knew I was loved by Garth and by God. My self-worth had been healthy. When Garth died so did my self-worth. I could not even prepare a meal without the fear that I would be inadequate to the task. I no longer experienced warm human love and I struggled also to experience God's love.

My relationship with God changed. The questions I first voiced at the time of Garth's death still lay unanswered: questions relating to the promises we were so sure he had made; promises of restoration, of wholeness for Garth personally and for the church. I held only broken dreams, promises and visions in my hands and I held God accountable for his failure to fulfil them. But that didn't fit my previous experience of God as faithful, loving and all powerful. So, instead, I held myself responsible for misinterpreting his Word. Either way trust died. I lost my open friendship with Jesus.

Friends called one day and shared how God had vindicated their faith in him. Their business had been in jeopardy. They abandoned it to God, as Abraham did with Isaac, and he gave it all back. 'He did not abandon us,' they said, with real conviction and joy.

I felt totally abandoned and in frustration I cried out, 'But I trusted Garth to God, I released him fully and he didn't give him back.' In tears of rage I fled to the bedroom, leaving confused friends wondering what they could do to help me.

Later I wrote to God:

I feel like Mary. She dedicated Jesus to you. She knew he was blessed of you. He lived and worked for you. She released him to you, saw his ministry grow, knew its power, saw the dead establishment challenged and new spiritual life beginning to grow. Suddenly it was all extinguished. You took him and he died. I feel like Mary must have – lost, angry and defeated.

My Will, Not Yours, Be Done

Yet, underneath it all I believe I trust you. It's an ambivalent feeling. As Peter questioned about his allegiance, I say, 'Who else can I go to? You have the words of eternal life.' I know that, but if there were someone else to go to I would. Lord God, help me to discover how Mary forgave and went on to the Resurrection. I need a resurrection of trust.

I heard the words of God as he called gently to me from Isaiah:

Come back and quietly trust in me. Then you will be strong and secure. (Isaiah 30:15)

He always does what is right. Happy are those who put their trust in the Lord. (Isaiah 30:18)

But I could not restore the trust myself. The words of the Lord had a hollow empty ring. Words I had quoted in the past to encourage belief in others bounced off my spirit. I longed for them to be pregnant with truth and life again.

While still in this ambivalent relationship with Jesus other losses loomed ahead. For eight happy years the manse and garden had been home to us. Yet they were not ours and they would be needed for a new minister. I had always reminded myself and the children that our home was a gift from God and one day we would move on and give it back to him with thanks. I hadn't anticipated the circumstances nor the depth of my attachment to those comfortable surroundings.

I first went house-hunting in April. The children and I prayed, drew up a list of our basic needs and committed the future to God. But the more houses I saw the more confused and despairing I became. I recognised some of my problem. Garth and I had always made major decisions together. Now the decision was all mine.

One day after seeing several houses, in frustration I stormed at the Lord. 'I don't want to go anywhere. This is home. I just want to stay right here.' The Lord listened. He let me rage. Later in the evening when all was quiet, the children in bed, I sat watching the dying embers of the fire and I asked, 'Lord, why am I so reluctant to move? Why can I find no house to please? Am I so difficult to satisfy?'

The answer he gave shattered me with its reality and pain. 'You are not happy with any of those houses, not because they are not lovely homes, but because they carry no footprints of Garth, nor ever will. You love this place because it is full of him.'

I saw it all. I saw him sitting in his chair against which I now leaned, his feet up on the mantelpiece, the coffee mug beside him, the paper on the floor. I saw the pictures he had hung, the table where he had sorted stamps and assembled model trains. I knew he would never be in our next home in this intimate way and I ached inside as I thought of a home without him. 'Lord, it hurts. Please take the pain, bind the wounds and set me free to live again in a home without him.'

He gave me his word from Psalm 90, verse 1: 'O, Lord, you have always been our home'. Not in a place, but in the Lord, would my home be.

The struggle to shift my security from the familiar (Garth, home, garden, ministry) to Jesus alone continued. As Jesus called me forth, I was shocked to realise how deep my roots were in the world. I was rooted in memories of Garth, my comfortable environment and familiar patterns of life. Jesus called me to be transplanted, rooted in him alone.

> Since you have accepted Christ Jesus the Lord live in union with him.
> Keep your roots deep in him. (Colossians 2:6, 7a)

I was busy one day packing Garth's study. As I sifted through mountains of paper two small sheets from his desk caught my attention. One read, 'Let Christ take root in your life'. A large deciduous tree illustrated the theme. There followed a prayer:

> Deep,
>   Deep within me
> The call,
>   The call of Christ

       Gentle, but strong;
Come, share my life,
       My prayer,
          My love,
              My obedience,
         My poverty,
     My mission.
Come if you will.
    Do not be afraid
       I AM WITH YOU.

The other sheet showed a fishing net, sandals and the words: 'Come Follow Me'. The prayer inside read:

Lord, as the fisherman trustingly casts his nets
into the depths of the sea,
so may I cast my life into the sea of your love
knowing that your tides
will draw me and your waves carry me
to the shores of my destiny.
As the sands surrender to the call of the sea,
so help me, Lord, to surrender to your call to me.
And they left their nets and followed him.

I was enmeshed in a net of security I had built. Again the Lord called me to follow him, to be rooted in him alone.

There, kneeling on the study floor, surrounded by piles of books and papers, I made those prayers my own and asked the Lord to help me to find my identity, worth, confidence, trust and security in him alone. I felt as I did when I first dived off the high board as a kid. The fear of letting toes uncoil off the edge of the board, plummeting into space, was the same fear I felt in Jesus' invitation. I still wanted to curl my fingers around the safe things. But he knew my heart. He led me on.

My house hunting continued. I was appalled at the tiny, modern sections, apologies for gardens. I longed for space and trees. Trees loomed large. I asked Jesus what they symbolised for me that I longed for them so much. I awoke from a dream with the answer. Trees had roots and long branches – arms of security. They were stable, providing shelter and privacy. My heart was crying out for stability and strong arms of love to embrace me, to hide my vulnerable emotions from the staring world. Again came the Lord's invitation to find all those things in him alone.

My packing continued. I was most distressed when packing Garth's study and his beloved model train set. I shared with the children the awful feelings I had as I boxed books and railway engines. It felt like boxing Garth and nailing him down forever. With wisdom beyond his years, Jim calmed my distress. He said, 'Dad is freer in heaven than he was here on earth. He's probably driving God's train into heaven. He always wanted to go back to driving trains. And he doesn't need his books any more. All his life he struggled to understand what God was all about. He tried to find the truth second-hand in books. But now that he is with God he will know all the truth. God will show him everything.'

Autumn settled into winter. The wind blew through the bare trees, the dying faded leaves piled up against the fence or swirled about in strong gusts of wind, their movement pointless. My emotions swirled in aimless motion as well, sometimes buoyed up, often dashed as they hit a wall of pain.

Katrina and a little friend spent wet days sewing lovely rag dolls. They were beautiful with lace trimmed skirts and frilly hats. It was fun. Her Dad would have loved to see her growing skills. Together we polished her swimming cups for that year, the last of which she had received the night before Garth died. Pride and pain mingled.

I settled by the fire one evening to enjoy the programme *25 Years of TV*. Clips from 1967 onward triggered off memories of events Garth and I had shared. They were foreign to my children. I realised with regret that I had a storehouse of memories that were now mine alone. I missed Garth so much.

Jesus alone shared my memories. Again the call to find everything in him reached my heart, but the sorrow was too strong for me to respond to his invitation.

My Will, Not Yours, Be Done

Ian poured himself into updating and organising his Dad's stamp collection which was now his. He found great joy in completing something his Dad had begun. The task lifted him from depression for a while, as did Christian camps which gave him something good to look forward to. His once open, warm nature gradually re-emerged. Then came a devastating school report: 'Ian doesn't concentrate'. 'Ian could do better'. And from the Dean, 'Not good enough, Ian!'

He was crushed. I was angry. Just four months had lapsed since Garth's death. Where was their sensitivity and understanding?

While I was still in a rage, Katrina arrived home upset. The teacher had asked her which parent was accompanying her on the cycle trip, Mum or Dad? 'He knew,' she sobbed, 'he knew Dad was dead.'

My anger intensified. I almost missed the Lord's warning: 'You must forgive one another just as the Lord has forgiven you' (Colossians 3:13b). I heard. But I felt justified in my anger and unwilling to obey.

That evening I shared my anger and pain with the Lord. Finally, I sought to forgive those who had wounded my children. Jesus met me. I felt his pain for them and for the wounds I carried. I felt him take it all. My anger dissolved in the light of his love. What freedom I experienced!

Forgiveness, it's wings to fly;
It's lightness, dance, uninhibited movement;
It's knowing you, Lord, close again;
It's knowing I carry nothing alone.
Yet when I bore it I remained alone.
When I gave up the bitterness
Then suddenly you seemed so near,
And the space was filled with peace and joy and love
Where only pain and anger had swirled in darkness.
The empty cross – you live.
Your power to save lives on.
I've tasted it. It's sweet and freeing.
I free Ian and Katrina also into your love .
For healing and life – your life in them.

I saw the teachers, but not in anger. The meeting was much more profitable and Ian went on to gain a glowing report later in the year, bounding in with the words, 'Dad would love this one.'

The Lord carried us in those months in amazing ways in spite of the fact that I spat at him like a trapped animal, often rejecting his consolation in favour of licking my own wounds. He kept presenting himself as loving, secure, consistent. He kept trying to restore my trust as I had asked him to.

In those tumultuous days I began to see God in a new way. In contrast to my own instability I saw the incredible stability of the Lord. Jesus was so secure in himself. He was never taken by surprise, never threatened. No-one caused his feelings, as others determined mine. He chose his own response out of his security and that response was always to love. I had felt the steady flow of that love through all my violent fluctuations.

My experience of God's love had gone through three transitions in my years of knowing him. I remembered firstly, as a young adult, when I thought *God loved me if I served him* and had right attitudes – if I proved myself somehow. Then I remembered vividly 1978 when that changed and I knew *he loved me just as I was*, for my sake. Oh, what freedom that brought. What joy! Now after weeks of raging, blaming, arguing, and lack of trust I knew *he loved me regardless of whether I was good, or utterly obnoxious*. I knew his constant love. It was absolutely amazing, a totally safe place to be.

You could be forgiven if you thought I could place myself in Jesus' security with ease. I couldn't. The struggle continued. The avalanche of losses snowballed. In the past I had found purpose, fulfilment and deep satisfaction in ministry. Now I had to deliberately let that role go, to free the church for a new ministry, a new manse family, new directions and new ways of doing things.

I hungered for the discussions Garth and I had shared; for the ministry we had fulfilled together. The manse felt so empty without Session meetings, callers, conversations with elders, parishioners, ministerial colleagues. I felt worthless. No task provided fulfilment. I described my lack of direction and purpose to Ian one day – a bit heavy for a fourteen-year-old, but frustration drove me to share about it. He listened, looked very thoughtful for a moment or two and then responded, 'I thought your purpose in life was to glorify God and to enjoy him forever. Dad's death hasn't changed that, has it?'

'Out of the mouths of babes...' Once again the Lord was saying, 'Look for the ultimates. You have focused on one expression of your purpose in life and it was good and right. But just as I changed your teaching career for one of ministry, I can provide a new vehicle for you in the future. Whatever form your work takes it does not alter its underlying goal. That remains the same and cannot be shaken.'

My goal was always to live to please God and to bring his love to others. With Ian's challenge I had to face up to the loss of the present expression of that goal, yet realise God would go on to redirect my resources to the same end in new ways, in his time. But for the moment it was emptiness; just one more loss.

More empty days led up to our wedding anniversary. I tried to cut out a jacket for Ian that day. The pattern needed adjusting in size and design. I marshalled all my determination and succeeded in the task, but was drained. The jacket was finished. I felt I was also. I pondered Jesus' words from the cross: 'It is finished' (John 19:30b).

I talked with Jesus:

When Garth died I had felt 'It is finished'. It seemed the end of life, vision, ministry, meaning and, almost, of belief. Yet Jesus, when you said those words yourself, it wasn't the end, it was the beginning. The church was born and countless people have found life through your death. I long to know and believe that life will grow out of Garth's death. I feel like the men on the road to Emmaus: confused, vision shattered; or like Peter: dejectedly fishing because all meaning had died with your death. Yet you met those men and Peter. You filled them with new hope. I need you to do that for me too.

The disciples had been unwilling to accept that the way to life was through Jesus' death. They resisted his move to Jerusalem and certain death. I had been unwilling to see that God's promise of wholeness for Garth included his death, that he might live. I had spurned the Scripture quoted to me: '…unless a grain of wheat fails into the earth and dies, it remains alone; but if it dies, it bears much fruit' (John 12:24 RSV).

I was equally unwilling to accept that the resurrection (the birth of hope, trust, purpose I sought within me) could only come about through a death – death to my will, surrender to his.

In a moment of intense grieving for Garth, I flicked through the Bible looking to read of Mary's grief. Perhaps there I could find understanding. Instead my eyes lighted on Mark 14:34. 'The sorrow in my heart is so great that it almost crushes me.' I knew all about that. I was crushed under sorrow and, like Jesus, I needed someone to watch with me.

I continued reading Mark 14. Suddenly I found myself watching with Jesus. I was in the garden as Jesus threw himself down on the ground crying, 'All things are possible for you. Take this cup of suffering from me' (Mark 14:36). I felt his deep cry. I was kneeling with him in the damp grass, experiencing his anguish, feeling the burden of his grief, tasting the bitter cup he was about to drink. The heaviness and bitterness of it was indescribable, beyond anything I had experienced in my own grief. It encompassed all my grief and all the brokenness of people in ages past. From the depths I heard him say, 'Yet not what I want, but what you want' (Mark 14:36). In awe I faced Jesus and whispered, 'How can you say such words? How can you accept this awful thing? How can you submit?'

I identified with Jesus' cry, 'The sorrow in my heart is so great that it almost crushes me' (Mark 14:34). I, like him, had thrown myself on the ground pleading with God to take away my cup of suffering because it was too bitter to drink. My cry, like his, had filled the silent night. I could identify with his deep desire to avoid suffering, but I could not in any way identify with him in that amazing statement of submission. I could not see how he had the power to do it.

Since that vivid awareness, I have seen others, like myself screech to a halt at that very same place and wrestle with the gulf between the deep desire to walk all the way with God, even to the cross of suffering, and the appalling realisation that they can't because the power of their own will is too strong.

My Will, Not Yours, Be Done

In prayer that night God had taken me out of my grief to let me experience Jesus' agony, taste his suffering and know his burning desire to avoid it, for it would cut him off from his Father. God let me discover the quality of Jesus' devotion. In spite of all Jesus felt and saw and feared he still said, 'Not my will, however, but your will be done' (Luke 22:42).

That night I met my rebellion face to face and saw its fearsome power; the power of 'I want', the power of *my will*. I was still saying:

Take this cup of suffering away from me.
Not your will but *mine* be done.

chapter
seven

COME ON OUT

'Let go. I'll catch you,' I had called to ten-year-old Ian as he dangled by one arm from the willow tree, body swinging above the tin fence. I'd heard his cry from the kitchen and had gone to him. Fear paralysed him. His fingers clung with vice-like grip to the slender branch. He wanted to be rescued. He couldn't bring himself to let go and trust me.

Now June 1985, four years later, God called to me, 'Let go. I'll catch you. Trust me.' I clung tenaciously and, like Ian, the more insecure I felt the more tightly I clung.

The words of the old hymn say:

On Christ the solid rock I stand.
All other ground is sinking sand.

I knew all about the sinking sand but I wasn't at all sure that Christ's rock hadn't sunk in that same shifting sand. I reached back for the rock of Garth's presence; the stability his love and life provided.

One day, longing for Garth's companionship, I looked up John 21. I immediately identified with Peter who filled his loneliness with the familiar – fishing. I entered the Bible passage in my imagination. I stepped

Shattered and Restored

out of the boat onto the cool wet sand and from a distance watched Jesus cooking fish. I became painfully aware of a set of footprints beside me in the sand. They were Garth's. I tried to step into them but mine didn't fit and I left no impression. I was anchored in my place and aching for the one I loved to fill those prints. Jesus called me to come to him, to step up the beach and eat with him. Instead I wept over the footprints. Then I became aware that the footprints went up the beach to Jesus. There they stopped. I had a choice to make: to sit with the empty prints or to step to Jesus. I wanted the prints to stay crystal clear; visible forever. My strong desire was to build a windbreak to protect them from the drifting sand. The Lord wanted me to leave them behind. There were new paths to walk, new prints to make.

It was some time later, through struggle and tears, that I stepped up to Jesus. He offered me fresh bread and newly cooked fish. I sat with the Lord in silence on a log and together we watched the drifting sand rounding the edge of the footprints, slowly filling them. I felt comfortable with Jesus. I knew I had wanted people to see the footprints Garth made. Yet he made them quite unconsciously while walking to Jesus. He wouldn't want people studying his prints. He always wanted people to meet with Jesus and to be fed by Jesus. It was best that the footprints fade, that the focus be on Jesus and what he was preparing for us, his people.

I came from that prayer time very aware of the Lord's deep love and his call to come to him. He had called me often in the past months. I'd always responded by reaching back to hold what wasn't there – the emptiness, the footprints, the memories. The Lord was warning me not to let precious memories, good gifts in themselves, trap me in the past. He called me to let go, to trust him to fill my hunger for companionship. He had heard my cry and had come to rescue me.

In Exodus we read that as the Israelite slaves in Egypt cried out to God, the Lord said to Moses:

> I have *seen* my people ... I have *heard* them cry out to be rescued ... I *know* all about their sufferings, and so I *have come* down to rescue them. (Exodus 3:7, 8 italics mine)

He did. Yet they too, in tough times, were trapped in their memories and grumbled to Moses:

> Did you have to bring us out here...?
> It would be better to be slaves there [in Egypt].
> (Exodus 14:11, 12)

What was God's response to their backward looking?

> Why are you crying out for help? Tell the people to move *forward*.
> (Exodus 14:15 italics mine)

The way out is through. For the Israelites the way out was through the wilderness, through learned obedience and battles to final victory.

In November 1984, just before we learned of Garth's cancer, I had the most vivid dream of my life. I dreamt I was turning the car in preparation for a journey. Garth called me to meet him in the church immediately. A red warning light flashed continuously on the corner of the garage. I followed Garth to the church where he spoke urgently of records being discovered in the city spelling doom to the Spanish. Fear gripped me. Suddenly we were reading Romans 8:38-39 together: 'For I am certain that nothing can separate us from the love of Christ, neither death nor life ... There is nothing in all creation that will ever be able to separate us from the love of God which is ours in Christ Jesus our Lord.' And peace replaced the fear.

I woke, the impression crystal clear, and recorded the dream in my diary, sure that God was trying to tell me something. I asked him to explain it. The red flashing light spoke of a warning. My positioning of the van signalled a new phase in my journey and it did not include Garth. His fear about the Spanish baffled me for a while. What did Spanish symbolise for me? Dance, joy, vibrant life. The fear was that it would all disappear from our lives and somehow there would be printed documents to that effect. But the overwhelming reaction was the promise from Romans 8 of the unfailing love of God.

Shattered and Restored

Two months later, as Garth struggled with illness and I struggled with fear, I shared the dream with a mature Christian friend. I understood much of the dream. I wanted to know where God was in the fear. My friend asked me to tell her where Jesus was in the dream. I recalled the dream and I found myself back in the church with Garth quoting God's promise of love. In my fear I wanted Jesus to express his love by sitting with us in the pew. I wanted his comforting presence. Instead I discovered he was on the cross, inviting me to 'Come on up'. I shrank from the suggestion of sharing his suffering.

Those words, 'Come on up', came back to me often in the months after Garth died. They were akin to the invitation to 'let go', the call on the beach 'to come' and the words from Isaiah 30:15, 'Come back and quietly trust in me'. Yet they said more. They were a call to acceptance of suffering as a way through to victory. Jesus' acceptance of the cross is our supreme example. Paul and James speak of being glad in trials and tribulations.

I heard the Lord's invitation long before I could reach that place of acceptance. I was still yearning for comfort, as a child with a skinned knee. But the word 'comfort' comes from the root 'forte' meaning 'strength'. There is a famous mural of William the Conqueror and his men in battle. He is prodding them on with a staff and underneath are the words, 'William comforteth his troops'. God's comfort is aimed at strengthening, giving dignity, independence, creativity and worth. Jesus' invitation to 'Come on up' was an invitation to be strengthened through the suffering, to be comforted in the true sense. He asked me to be willing, as he was when he accepted the cup of suffering and his Father's will.

I heard the invitations. I had felt comfortable with Jesus on the beach. I had let go some things – Garth, ministry, dreams, plans. The ground I stood on shrank. A major leap of trust was required. But I was paralysed as Ian had been in the willow tree. The paralysis was fear.

I feared a new future alone. I feared I would be unable to give my children the stability and direction they needed. I feared the responsibility of all the choices being on my shoulders. I was afraid that I couldn't make a wise choice of house. I feared failure. And I even feared to trust God with my fears.

Two years before, in fear at the responsibility of leading in a retreat, I found the Lord delivered me through prayer. Psalm 34:4 had come true for me in a powerful way.

I prayed to the Lord and he answered me;
he freed me from all my fears.

I turned again to Scripture for God's answer to fear and to rediscover what I had always known:

For the spirit that God has given us does not make us timid...
(2 Timothy 1:7)
(It is the human spirit which trembles.)

The truth will set you free. (John 8:32)
(When I discover the truth again.)

The power working in us is the same as the mighty strength which he used when he raised Christ from death. (Ephesians 1:19, 20)
(If only I could release it.)

I am sure he is able to keep safe till that Day what he has entrusted to me. (2 Timothy 1:12)

I knew it. But where was the power to do it? June came and went. July, cold and wet. The trees stood bare and dormant, no visible sign of life, naked to the elements, waiting, waiting for the warm rays of spring sunshine to call forth new buds and tender green shoots.

I waited also, feeling just as naked and vulnerable. Caring folk asked if I had chosen a house. How could I tell them I was afraid to? How could I voice my fears? I wandered in the garden one day. Tepid wintry sun bathed the scene. The warm sweet humus of autumn's death scented the air. I bargained with the Lord, 'If I have to move from this beloved place and begin a new life, at least show me a view of it. Give me something to step into. Show me your plan.' Back came his answer: 'Step into me alone. I am all you need.'

Into my mind sprang a well known and loved quote from *The Unknown Way* by M. Louise Haskins:

> I said to the man who stood at the gate of the year, 'Give me a light that I may tread safely into the unknown.' And he replied, 'Go out into the darkness and put your hand into the hand of God. That shall be to you better than light and safer than a known way.'

Those words sounded lovely in Christian devotions. They sounded scary that wintry afternoon as I finally faced the reality that I had to let go. But knowing and doing were two different things. My sense of powerlessness heightened. I had moved from saying, 'I won't' (the stage in grief commonly called denial), to saying, 'I'm willing but I can't'. I identified with Lazarus; bound, entombed, on the verge of a whole new existence, but still not free. I knew there was new life within me, even as the life surges hidden within the bare branches of a tree in late winter, or as a caterpillar wriggles in its cocoon after weeks of dormancy; but I still didn't know how to break out.

I voiced my dilemma to a beautiful Catholic sister whom I had met previously on retreat and in whose quiet convent I had found the space and peace, on numerous occasions, to hear the Lord above my stormy emotions. I drew the parallel between myself and Lazarus. Marleen listened attentively. She suggested I use that Scripture passage, put myself in Lazarus' place and see what the Lord would say to me.

I found a sunny step, leaned back against the warm wall, asked God to meet me in his Word and began to read slowly from John 11. Lazarus was ill. I'd been ill too, with a broken heart, and a wounded spirit. Lazarus' family sent for Jesus. Hope welled within me at his words: 'The final result of this sickness will not be the death of Lazarus; this has happened in order to bring glory to God, and it will be the means by which the Son of God will receive glory' (John 11:4).

Yet Jesus stayed away. I lay in my darkness and I waited, angry that he didn't come. Finally, I appeared dead. Certainly trust, hope and faith had died, all the things that give a person real life, and they buried me.

Friends came to mourn. I recognised headmasters from my past who mourned the death of my teaching gift. My children came with their sports gear mourning my death to joy, fun, spontaneity. Friends came mourning my death to freedom, creativity, self-worth, confidence. Then came some folk I had ministered to after Garth's death. They moved among the mourners saying, 'But she's not dead. I live because of her.' They knew that under the bindings I was still alive. I knew that too.

Jesus arrived. He told Mary and Martha I would rise. I thought, 'I'll believe it when I see it.'

I wanted to say Amen to those who said, 'He gave sight to the blind. Could he not have kept Elsa from dying?' The Lord ordered my mourners to remove the stone. The light flooded in. Jesus called to me, 'Come out.' To my amazement I argued, 'But I'm bound, Lord. Can't you see that? Come in and unwrap me. I can see and hear, but I can't move. Do something.' Jesus remained at the doorway and repeated the invitation, 'Come on out, Elsa.'

'Lord, if I come out in my own strength I'll just go right back in again. I can't stay free. I just get bound up again so quickly. I can't sustain freedom. There is no flow of life, just a pulling-myself-up-by-my-bootlaces and pretty soon I trip over them and crash again. Where is your power to free?'

I'm always amazed at the things God reveals when I go to his Word and apply it to myself. I saw my challenge to Jesus to exercise his power. I saw my fear. But I was still stuck. I shared my frustration with Marleen. She prayed that God would show me what blocked my response to Jesus' invitation. I could go no further that day. I had to return to my children and the tasks at home.

Later that week I met with two friends whose Christian wisdom and gentle nature I trusted. In the quiet sanctuary of the church I unfolded my struggle and the impasse I had reached with the Lord. We prayed seeking the light of revelation. The words of Joshua came to me:

Shattered and Restored

> I have commanded you to be determined and confident! Don't be afraid or discouraged, for I, the Lord your God, am with you *wherever* you go. (Joshua 1:9 italics mine)

He did not chide me for my fear. He understood and promised his presence with me in the wherever I was so scared of. We sat on in silent prayer. Carol broke the silence: 'I sense the Lord is asking you to leave some things behind in the tomb, then you will be free to come out.'

'But what, Lord?' Into my spirit came the words: 'Your house will be my home as long as I live' (Psalm 23:6).

I understood Jesus' call to leave in the tomb the ground I called home, to close the door on it and to move from denial and bargaining back into Jesus alone. He would be my home. It seemed like a dead end, shutting the last door, with none open in front. When Jesus faced the cross it must have felt the same, leaving behind all, not knowing the next scene. Jesus' trust in his Father was vindicated. Mine would be also.

In the loving presence of Carol and Ann, I handed back to Jesus all I had known and loved and finally let go my clinging grasp and transferred my trust to him.

Having prayed, we returned to the scene of the tomb and Jesus with renewed confidence that some progress would now be possible. I had already a measure of freedom in my spirit. We lapsed again into silence. In my spirit I saw the Lord at the entrance of the tomb. I heard again his call, 'Come on out.'

'Empty words,' I argued. 'Use your power.' Suddenly, in that moment, the Spirit showed me the other major problem. I would never have guessed it. It took God's light to reveal it. I saw with amazing clarity the human words that had been spoken to me. Garth in his illness had said, 'If I die all God's promises are vain and empty.' After Garth's death some frustrated, hurting parishioners had said to me, 'If you had prayed believing, he would not have died.'

Those words surfaced in my mind. I realised I had received them into my spirit and they had hindered my openness to the Lord's Word and shaken my trust in him. They had brought death, not life, to my spirit, because they were not words of truth. Right there I forgave those who spoke them to me. I asked forgiveness for accepting them. I left them in the tomb, renouncing them forever.

The Holy Spirit flashed passages of the Bible across my mind to show me the power of the Word, Jesus' word:

And God *said* 'Let there be light...' (Genesis 1:3 NIV italics mine)

The *Word* was the source of life... (John 1:4 italics mine)

So he *said* to the paralysed man, 'Get up, pick up your bed, and go home'. (Matthew 9:6b italics mine)

'The *words* I have spoken to you bring God's life-giving Spirit.' (John 6:63b italics mine)

Then [Jesus] got up and *ordered* the winds and the waves to stop, and there was a great calm. (Matthew 8:26b italics mine)

So [Jesus] *said* to the fig tree, 'You will never again bear fruit!' At once the fig tree dried up. (Matthew 21:19b italics mine)

He ... sustains the universe with his powerful *word*.
(Hebrews 1:3 KJV italics mine)

The *word* of God is alive and active, sharper than any two-edged sword. (Hebrews 4:12a italics mine)

As these passages flowed through my mind, I grasped anew the enormous power of God's Word. In the tomb I heard him say, 'Come on out.' The power to come out was in the spoken invitation. I came out, not in my strength, but in the power of his *living Word*. With his command he always gives the enabling. The word and the power are one.

I will remember always the freedom of that prayer time, and the precious friends who entered my struggle, faithfully listened to God and shared my joy.

Years ago I had discovered something of the power of words. I saw parents destroy their children's egos with words. 'You're dumb'. You're hopeless'. 'You'll never be any good'. I've seen lovely people speak a word of encouragement that brought life to a struggling soul and healing to a wounded spirit. We need to be so careful that the words we speak are words of life. We need also to recognise those words that have brought death and destruction to us and to renounce them, receiving in their place the words of truth, the words of Jesus, that bring life and freedom.

I left the church knowing the struggle had not ended; the pain of saying goodbye still ahead of me, but with a new freedom and a deepened trust in my God. I had let go and found his everlasting arms!

There was one further thing I wanted to do; to leave our home in gratitude. So I wrote a Thank You letter to the Lord.

For all this I give you thanks, Lord

For your trust in us to build your temple in St Paul's.
For this warm and cosy home, just fine for our children,
    with space to play in summer and warm fireside in winter.
For the garden already created by loving hands.
For the huge willow; fun for children to climb.
For the developing fernery, its quiet coolness and bushy smell.
For rain shining on wet leaves and fantails flitting through the fronds.
For spring nests, the baby fantails, the grey warbler and
    goldfinches growing and hidden by fat red plums.
For soft pink carpets of cherry blossom and red autumn leaves.
For picnics and barbecues; children racing through the garden,
    cycling under the trees.
For hands laden with garden produce and children raiding raspberries
    crisp new apples and sweet young peas.
For the labour of building together stone walls and garden fences,
    animal homes and a tree hut for the children.

Come On Out

For many refreshing, quiet lunchtimes together outside,
>   soaking in the peace, sunlight and shadows.

For fun things like bedtime stories outside on summer evenings,
>   cricket games that extended over church and house;
>   for the clothes line that doubled as a merry-go-round.

For birthday parties, lollies hidden in model trains.

For cycle races around the church, treasure hunts, gymnastics on the
>   verandah rails, and hockey on the front lawn.

For a garden full of toddlers watching chooks, shredding silver beet
>   for Skuttles, the guinea pig, and tucking tiny rabbits up jerseys.

For the carefully placed stones that remind us of Skuttles and our cat,
>   who lived and died and were a part of us here.

For the sunny sandpit (filled with trucks, cranes and eager little boys)
>   now abandoned and used for potting mix.

For times spent with Garth as he built model trains
>   and drove them with the boys.

For house painting and watching our growing boys
>   up painting the roof.

For the shared heartaches and joys of ministry;
>   for praise services, celebrations, prayer times of power and unity,
>   watching people grow in Jesus.

For wonderful friends who shared our home, enjoyed our children,
>   kept us company and encouraged us.

For session meetings and prayer times, suppers and fellowship times,
>   music group, children burning up energy on the trampoline,
>   and large boys coming and going, filling the space with noise
>   and movement and always emptying the refrigerator.

Lord, a thousand memories I carry and I thank you for each one.
>   You blessed us richly. You will continue to do so.
>   With deep gratitude I acknowledge your gift and release it for you
>   to bring rich blessing to another of your choice.

We move on with you to a new set of memories,
>   just waiting to be made.

My new freedom gave me the confidence to buy a house and so began the mammoth task of packing seventeen years of accumulated possessions. The night before we were due to shift, surrounded by packing cases and warmed by a cosy fire, my children and I spent some time listing the precious memories we would carry with us and for which we wanted to give thanks. We read them to each other. How many there were! Things I had forgotten. Sleeping in the tree hut under the stars, raising the tiny shining cuckoo, cookouts in the dark with charcoaled faces, making music together in the church in the evenings, reading stories by the fire, and many more. What a rich tapestry the Lord had helped us to weave. We were sure he would help us to weave a new one.

That night we prayed together and read Psalm 16, a prayer of confidence in our God, as we left the past behind.

> You, Lord, are all I have,
> and you give me all I need;
> my future is in your hands.
> How wonderful are your gifts to me.
> (Psalm 16:5, 6a)

chapter

eight

PLEASE JESUS, DON'T DIE

On 19 October 1985, exactly eight years after we had arrived as a complete family in Feilding, we moved house. In distance it was a short move – just two blocks away. Emotionally it was a quantum leap. The morning dawned clear and sunny, spring fragrance filled the air. Ian wandered slowly through the old garden, stopping to gaze silently at favourite corners. I watched him from the kitchen window, a lump in my throat, knowing he was drinking it all in, longing to keep it, having as much difficulty as I to let it go. We had come full of expectation and promise. We had experienced fun times and the Lord's blessing in this place. We left with broken dreams and without Garth, to face scary new beginnings.

Soon we were caught up in the activity as willing helpers from our church family shuttled back and forth, transferring our belongings to our new house. I found it impossible, needing to be in both houses at once, to supervise loading and delivering. 'Garth, why aren't you here?' I chided silently. 'It would be so much easier.' But then we wouldn't need to shift if he were with us. I swallowed the pain and busied myself, directing furniture to new positions, finding bedding for the ladies who made it possible for us to rest in comfortable beds at the end of an exhausting day. I will remain forever grateful for the enormous support I

Shattered and Restored

received in practical ways from my church family. Two years later, my sons, now strong 16-year-olds, helped a solo Mum and two children move house. In tears, she had shared that she didn't know how she would manage alone. I thought back to the hive of activity the day we shifted – the strong men with trailers, the women with meals, the beds made and kitchen cupboards organised by loving hands.

That night, as I soaked away the exhaustion in a hot bath, I experienced a flash of joy – the strong awareness of God's presence with me, in our new home. I had been surrounded by love all day. My defences had melted and I recognised God. I wrote of it in my diary.

> You don't miss many opportunities to say 'I love you', do you, Lord? Today I heard you and could respond. Lord, thank you for the richness of today; for precious memories from the past. We have much to praise you for. Help us to build a new, rich bank of memories right here. Fill our home and lives with your peace and joy. Give us a measure of your creative nature to plan fun things together and to share ourselves with others. It's exactly eight years since I sat in the manse kitchen and cried at the stack of boxes and the work ahead of us. New beginnings scare me, Lord, yet you have promised to be with us and you call me to trust that promise. You said, 'I would go out with joy, be led forth with peace.' Yesterday I couldn't see how it could be. Yet it is so and my heart sings. I know that even though sad times come, there will be singing again. Joy cannot die because it is your life in me.

The joy was like a shaft of light through a window into heaven, a fleeting tantalising glimpse.

Morning dawned. The window to heaven slammed shut. The light extinguished. I woke in a new place. It didn't feel like home. It didn't sound like home. Barking dogs had broken my sleep. The trees rustled differently. The smells were different. The house echoed, concrete floors bouncing the sounds back. We couldn't find anything we needed and we fell over each other in the small dinette. Ian and I, so used to retreating to the church for quiet times with God, hunted in vain for a quiet, private corner. There was none, neither inside nor outside. The smaller garden was visible from the dining room and lounge windows, and neighbours surrounded us on all sides. I retreated to my room, but with a double bed in a 2.7m x 3.7m room there was no feeling of space. Claustrophobia engulfed me and I left again.

In the weeks that followed, I was dogged by weariness, restlessness, disorientation, crushing loneliness and increasing depression. I threw my questions to the Lord.

> If this home is right for us, why am I so restless? Why do I experience no peace? Why does the manse seem so right and this so wrong? Why can't I experience your confirmation? What are you saying about it? I miss Garth here. I miss the manse. I miss the morning teas with the office staff. But Lord, I miss you, too. Where are you? Why am I so confused and tearful? Why can't I sustain a positive outlook? Why am I so ungrateful for what is really a beautiful home? Where is the peace I once knew in you?

My questions bounced right back unanswered and the darkness deepened. As I worshipped in the church next door to the manse, my heart longed to be back there in its quiet restful setting. I couldn't stay a full day in our new home. Each day I went out walking, visiting, shopping – anything to escape the feeling of isolation and depression.

After one particularly dreadful day, I wrote to the Lord: 'Without hope, even the light places become dark.'

During this time of struggle, I called again on my Catholic sister friend, needing her wisdom, gentleness and direction. We sat together in the sun. She listened attentively as I poured out my frustration. An occasional question from her clarified my thinking, and comments from time to time assured me that she understood and cared. She prayed with me and suggested that I spend time alone in the chapel before the cross on which Jesus hung in pain for me, and meet him there.

The chapel was so silent. I sat a long time looking at the crucifix, then looking at Mary, reading the expression on her face. I felt I stood alongside

Shattered and Restored

John and Mary on that Calvary hill as the awful event happened. I felt Mary's pain. She bore him, watched him grow, had a vision of his powerful ministry (expressed in the Magnificat), and it was all dying before her eyes. Man's greed, hate, power and sin had killed him. He was dead. Garth was dead, too, and God had stood by and let it happen to Garth, as to Jesus. I knew some of Mary's pain. It was mine, too. I watched Jesus die on the cross, and I felt him dying in me, too. Peace and joy and truth had died, and trust also. I seemed reduced to my human resources.

I prayed, 'Jesus, I am hungry for your life in me. Please Jesus, don't die. I couldn't bear it. Live, please live in me. I feel so separated from you.' I heard the cry of my heart, 'They have taken my Lord, and I don't know where he is.'

In the stillness of the chapel, I realised the depths of my longing for Jesus and my grief at our broken relationship. I felt as the psalmist must have, in Psalm 42.

> As a deer longs for a stream of cool water,
> so I long for you, O God.
> I thirst for you, the living God.
> When can I go to worship in your presence?
> Day and night I cry,
> and tears are my only food…

> My heart breaks when I remember the past,
> when I went with the crowds to the house of God
> and led them as they walked along…

> To God, my defender, I say,
> 'Why have you forgotten me?'
> …they keep asking me, 'Where is your God?'

Jesus was the answer. But I didn't know Jesus in me any more. I remember after Garth died, his absence was so intense that his image never left me, making the loss all the more poignant. It felt the same with Jesus. I missed his presence. His absence intensified the memory of his once present reality. I couldn't fathom why attempts to meet Jesus always triggered tears and a deep sense of loss. It was the same as moments when I focused on Garth. I wept at the loss of all that had been so real, warm and sustaining. I was in grief for both of them. The only prayer on my lips was 'Jesus'. I wanted to cling to the truth of his Word, which says, 'I will never leave you.' I needed to believe it was true. But I feared it was not. As I had earlier doubted his power and love, I began to doubt his Word also. That was really scary. Into the emptiness, I prayed with the words of the psalm:

> Give me life, so that I may praise you...
> I wander about like a lost sheep;
> so come and look for me, your servant.
> (Psalm 119:175, 176)

But the darkness deepened. The silence continued. The days were full, hectic with end-of-year activities, school functions and planning for a six-week South Island holiday to see family and friends. Joyfully, we had prepared for this trip two years ago, then abandoned it because of Garth's health. Now, tensely, I made preparations, very aware of our incompleteness. I was exhausted, unsure of my planning, and fearful of coping with long days of driving, which Garth would have enjoyed. I dreaded backing our big van onto the ferry for the trip between Islands. I was apprehensive about meeting friends and travelling to familiar places where, previously, Garth and I had always been together. The loneliness and fear gripped me. I was hopeful it would be healing, otherwise I would not have undertaken such a trip. Yet it would be painful. Christmas would bring mixed feelings: joy at being together with my parents, three sisters, their husbands and children, and an awareness of the gap left by Garth's death. The stress reached a climax just before we set out on our trip. The hectic preparations and weariness precipitated an argument with the children. I handled the situation badly, and in despair, withdrew to my room. With no one to share my feelings, I wrote to the Lord:

Shattered and Restored

God, I feel utterly alone. Who will comfort me? I long for Garth's arms safe around me and I'm lost and lonely and utterly broken. I've yelled at the kids, failed to hear Katrina's news and wounded her deeply. Lord, I've lashed out at all of them. I feel so guilty. I hate myself and my own worthlessness. I see others with competence, faith and hope. I have neither self-confidence nor confidence in you. All I have left is a broken set of dreams and shattered hopes, and faith has died. I feel utter despair. Folk say you can work with a broken person. Well, they don't come more broken than I, and I hope you're satisfied. Do you take delight in breaking, moulding and pushing people through pain and despair?

Where are you? What do you care? Does power really belong to you? Are you praised by my brokenness? How? I can't see it. Despair. Depression. They do not speak of you.

Nothing speaks of you right now. I've lost you in me. You need to be born in me this Christmas and I can't do that.

chapter

nine

PROMISE OF RESTORATION

With an empty space in the van where Garth once sat, and an empty place in my heart where Jesus once lived, we drove the long, hot journey home for Christmas. The days were beautiful, the countryside magnificent in summer dress. Friends welcomed us, gave us a night's rest and sent us on, refreshed and loved.

Sitting by the roaring Buller River, watching its determined movement to reach the sea, I recalled the dream I had before Garth died when, together in the church, we had read the words of Romans 8:

> For I am certain that nothing can separate us from his love: neither death nor life ... there is nothing in all creation that will ever be able to separate us from the love of God which is ours through Christ Jesus our Lord. (Romans 8:38–39)

I let the words wash over my spirit and gouge away at my doubts as this living river cut away the barriers between itself and the mighty ocean.

Walking a bushtrack in the Lewis Pass, the canopy of trees touching overhead, I heard the words: 'He is near to those who are discouraged; he saves those who have lost all hope' (Psalm 34:18). As the trees entwined,

I longed to embrace my Lord and for him to hold me in his arms.

Walking by a stony riverbed, exploring the driftwood for interesting pieces, I came across a twisted piece, worn and bleached, a long way from its source. Once a living tree, now it lay, battered and dead, tossed by the waters, worn by the stones, yet strangely beautiful. I thought of Jesus in death; torn, worn and battered by evil, and feeling as abandoned as the twisted driftwood. His cry echoed in my spirit, 'My God, why have you abandoned me?' Yet, in the very next breath, he could say, 'Into your hands I place my spirit.' I marvelled. He still wanted to place his spirit into the Father's hands in spite of feeling utterly abandoned by him. He knew there was no other place. I picked up the driftwood. Could I trust God that much? I needed Jesus' level of confidence, but I didn't have it any more.

Christmas was a joyous time. All twenty-three of us celebrated Jesus' birth. We worshipped in the local church. It was good to be together in worship with my family. I had first met Garth in this church and I missed him there. Pain pierced the joy, as it would do again and again on this holiday. We feasted outside in brilliant sunshine, opened gifts, laughed and joked. My children renewed friendships with cousins and grandparents. It was a joyful day and I felt the Lord's arms embrace me through my family.

Then in bed that night, glad in heart, suddenly a wave of loneliness swept over me. The loss of Garth, more intense than for many days, brought tears of sadness. I focused on the good things of the day and finally peace replaced the sorrow. Good times, drowned in waves of sorrow, were a regular occurrence and had been for months.

Friends trying to console me said, 'Time will heal.' I doubted the wisdom of that statement. I have seen people grow bitter, resentful and angry with time. With time, their wounds have festered and poisoned body, mind and spirit. They are people we avoid because their bitterness flows out and contaminates all of life. Others, with time, have grown gentle and compassionate. Their wounds have healed, the memory remaining to keep them loving and sympathetic to others' pain. The treatment the wound gets determines whether time will bring healing or hate.

The lazy summer holidays, the love of family and friends and the beautiful South Island scenery, all combined to form a salve for my wounds. They spoke peace to my stormy emotions till, in the calm, God could speak and I could hear.

I sat by the cool waters of the Kyeburn stream one hot, lazy summer afternoon talking with Valerie while the children cooled off in the water hole at the river bend. She asked me about my relationship with Jesus. I was embarrassed. I could not tell her it was good. I wanted to, but it wasn't true. I tried to describe what had happened. I drew illustrations from life to help her understand something beyond her experience.

My relationship with Jesus felt like a broken marriage, where trust, once strong, has been destroyed. In deep heartache, the two have nothing to say to each other and can't rebuild the shattered trust, yet they hunger for the love and satisfaction they once knew. I felt that way about Jesus. I had loved and trusted him, but that trust lay in tatters at my feet, and though I longed to re-establish it, somehow I couldn't do it. I was in a vicious circle, needing to experience his love, to feel secure enough to trust him again, yet knowing that I could never experience that love without first trusting myself to him. How does one break that circle? I had no idea. I wept as I shared with Valerie my frustration with prayer and my desire to know again Jesus' love for me. As the psalmist wrote:

> I felt secure and said to myself, 'I will never be defeated.'
> You were good to me, LORD;
> you protected me like a mountain fortress.
> But then you hid yourself from me, and I was afraid.
> (Psalm 30:6, 7)

> Do not take your Holy Spirit away from me.
> Give me again the joy of your salvation.
> (Psalm 51:11, 12)

> O, God, you are my God, and I long for you.
> My whole being desires you;

> like a dry, worn out, and waterless land,
> my soul is thirsty for you.
> (Psalm 63:1)

I had time and space in which to pray, with my children fully occupied with cousins, exploration, swimming, or just lazing. Prayer still seemed utterly futile. Day after day, I tried to talk with Jesus. Each attempt just highlighted his absence. One morning, in total frustration, I abandoned the effort in favour of a walk. If Jesus wasn't going to meet me, I reasoned, I could make better use of my time and get some much needed exercise.

The pace I set was fast and furious. The stones crunched under my feet. The wind blew the hair off my face and stung my eyes. They were already watering with tears of frustration. I needed Jesus so much. I crunched my frustration underfoot, stomped my way along the well-worn sheep tracks. After some distance, I began to puff with exertion. The land was hilly and rugged; scarred remains of gold mining days. The track edged its way around cliffs, down scree slopes to deep gullies, along streambeds and up the face of another scarred hillside. Eventually, weariness tempered my frustration. I slowed and gave more attention to the scene around me.

It was quite beautiful – deep yellow cliffs, topped with tussock and self-sown larch trees of soft green, contrasting with the dark green pine trees, and framing it all, the distant blue hills of the Hawkden Range, still with patches of snow in shady gullies. I sat and rested on the springy ground cover, leaning my back against the slender trunk of a larch tree. I ran the carpet of warm gold-coloured needles through my fingers. Tiny native plants at my feet caught my attention; little star-like pink flowers on tall stems, tiny bluebells I remembered from childhood, a creeping blue plant with broad wrinkly rust-coloured leaves, and a myriad of other plants had covered the ochre-coloured ground, laid bare by the mining. I drank it in: the beauty of it, the peace, the silence. Tiny, noiseless moths, and native butterflies fluttered from flower to flower, or rested, wings folded, on a waving blade of grass.

The Lord broke the silence. Not with words, but he spoke deep in my spirit, stilled for this brief moment by the beauty and peace.

One hundred years ago, the thirst for money drove miners to rape this country for gold. They tore the hillsides apart, broke up the rolling tussock-country into jagged cliffs and stony wasteland. It was scarred and ugly, devoid of plant life. They left it naked and raw. I recalled, as a child, sliding down the scree slopes from the cliff top, collecting coloured stones from the streambed, hunting for rabbit burrows in the exposed hillsides, and trekking home in the blazing heat, little rabbits tied up in cardigan sleeves. There was no shelter from the heat or dust, and the sun reflected off the jagged cliffs and yellow wasteland. My life, too, had been torn apart, left raw and ugly, with jagged edges and deep gullies of despair.

Yet, as I sat and drank in the scene, I was acutely aware that it had been restored – reclothed in great beauty. Magnificent trees stretched to the blue Central Otago sky, thousands of them, leaving only patches of bare, steep cliff face, contrasting with the soft green of the trees. There was cool shelter in their shade. The stony remains of sluicing were covered with lichens, mosses, grasses and native plants. Birds had found a haven and sang their praises. The whole scene was alive with growth and was truly beautiful. I felt God speak:

> These hills have sat here for one hundred years. They have not struggled to be restored. I, the Lord, have done it. I will do it for you also. Just rest in me and watch. I will restore you also. I am in the restoration business. It is my nature.

I saw, too, that deep wounds, like the mining and my loss of Garth, leave gaping holes and jagged scars. The hole would not be filled. It would remain forever different, but it could become truly beautiful, more beautiful than the original state.

A quiet hope filled my breast. A warm peace settled upon me. I tasted joy for the first time in months, savouring it as a child with a special sweet. Jesus was not dead. He was alive and active in this landscape and also in me, doing what he did best, restoring broken things.

I sat in silence, absorbing the scene, letting every sense record it. I saw the narrow sheep tracks along which I had stomped. They, too, spoke to me. Nothing grew on them. No seed could survive there. I saw my thought patterns as those tracks, hard beaten as I moved in endless circles of destructive negative thoughts. There, resting under the larch tree, I asked the Lord to help me break the beaten tracks in my mind. I asked his help to rest in him while he restored me in his time. I walked often after that, not struggling to pray, just taking in the beauty and thanking Jesus for it.

Another morning, very early, I sat by a beautiful dam, created during the mining days as a water reservoir. Yellow with sediment at that time, now it was clear blue and full of trout. The mist rose off the water, a fish fed among the weeds, birds called from the soft green foliage of trees growing by the dam, and a rabbit came near to feed. It was a scene of total harmony. It spoke of being and, especially, of being still. It spoke, too, of the Lord who never changes; the Lord who was, and still is, the same. There was a stability, like an anchor in a storm, in knowing that the Lord who had blessed me with health, children, Garth, friends and love, would not change either his blessings or his nature.

Yet, a restlessness crept into me. I wanted so badly to hear from the Lord. I was impatient to be restored. I still found it hard to rest; to await God's timing; to live with the silence and the lack of communication with Jesus that had grown out of my broken trust. The hills were inviting me to trust him. My wounded emotions were still saying, 'He's not trustworthy. It's all an illusion. He'll only hurt you more.'

I sat on, reflecting on truths that had come to me in the past in this same quiet spot. Five years before, after a hectic, exhausting year of ministry, we had come here to my parents' place to holiday. During the preceding days, travelling down the beautiful New Zealand west coast, I had experienced Jesus' presence often, yet felt guilty for not praying regularly for St. Pauls folk and parish needs. I vowed I would do so when settled at Naseby. Before dawn, I had risen and walked to the dam with the specific intention of praying. The morning was glorious. A stillness crept over me. I sat absorbed in the beauty; the reflections as clear as the cliffs and trees themselves. The sun had risen silently from behind the hills and cast a golden glow over the scene. A duck glided across the water, leaving ripples that caught the sunlight, and shattered the reflections. God's world was so beautiful. My heart had filled with praise to him. Then I remembered I had come to pray. But my prayer, as I planned it, never came about. Into my spirit came the words of Jesus, not audible but as a clear knowing. 'Do not strive. I am interceding for my people before the Father. Just rest and enjoy me for now.'

This morning, five years later, impatient, restless for progress, I remembered his call to rest, to enjoy him. I remembered also the words of Corrie Ten Boom: 'Don't wrestle. Just nestle.' This morning the reflections were perfect. I thought of the dam as it used to be, yellow with sediment, reflecting nothing. As the sediment settled over time, the water cleared. On a still day it was possible to see the coloured stones on the bottom of the dam and the reflections on the water's surface. If I could but rest and let the sediment inside me settle a while, maybe I would see more clearly and catch the reflection of Christ again in my stilled soul.

On Sunday, I sat with my family in the little local church. That morning, the General Assembly banner was pinned along one wall. The minister explained the symbolism in it, the story behind it, and that it was to be displayed in all Presbyterian churches in New Zealand during the year. As the service progressed, I looked at the banner. A rainbow was painted the full length of it. It was not painted as the usual arch, but as a ribbon of seven colours which twisted and turned, sometimes full view with all colours showing, sometimes at a turn, narrow, just one colour remaining. The rainbow spoke to me of hope. God had planted a little hope in my life as I sat under the larch tree. I had known times in the past of confident hope and the broad ribbon spoke of those times when the faith walk was easy. The narrow corners of ribbon reflected the diminished hope and tottering faith walk of the moment. Yet, it only looked a narrow point, because of the angle of viewing. The ribbon in reality was always the same width. Hope is in God who doesn't change, who is not diminished by our view of him and, once again, I felt his encouragement. My appreciation of his nature was being restored. The only colour that ran unbroken the full length of the rainbow ribbon was red. It spoke to me of the blood of Jesus; the thread that holds it all together. I sensed

God's invitation to come back to the cross, somehow, and quietly trust in him. I have no recollection of the sermon for that day. For me, God had his message in a painted ribbon rainbow. His message: 'I am your Lord. I do not change. Trust me. I am restoring you.' He repeated that message again and again in those six weeks of holiday and a ray of light, a shaft of hope began to pierce the gloom. God was in the business of restoration. He really cared. I received his promise that one day I would be whole.

chapter

ten

THE EMPTY TOMB

Someone once said to a friend in deep grief, 'In suffering, you can choose either to sink or swim. It will be better for all of us if you choose to swim.'

After the holiday, I felt that at least I was floating, but returning to Feilding was like shooting me over the Niagara Fails, and as the waters of despair tumbled over me, I lost my buoyancy and feared I would drown. Life rafts of love, thrown by friends, kept my head above the torrent for short periods. The promise of resurrection and restoration given by God in the hills at Naseby and in the rainbow banner acted as a lifeline, assuring me I was held by God, even in the turbulence. Once, long ago, I had a poster with the words, 'When you get to the end of the rope, tie a knot and hang on'. Somehow, the promise God had given me in January assured me that the outcome was not dependent on my ability to hang on. The fact was that God held on to me and he was not about to let go. I may be tossed about, submerged at times, but never drowned because my God, who loves me, is faithful to his Word. He said, 'I will never leave you; I will never abandon you' (Hebrews 13:5b).

When we first moved into our new home I put up two important posters to focus on. One was of magnificent spring blossoms, with the words, 'God never makes a mistake'. I had bought it before Garth became ill, and later challenged its truth. Yet, I wasn't prepared to throw it away. I needed to rediscover the truth it stated. The other was of a little kitten, fast asleep in a flower pot. Underneath were the words, 'If you are at peace in yourself any place is home'. I had bought that poster deliberately when I felt so lost and uprooted in our new setting. I read it often, with a prayer to God that it might come true. It reminded me that the restlessness could not be blamed on the house or the children. It could not be projected outside of myself. The turmoil was within and, therefore, nowhere would I feel at home until it was stilled.

When we arrived back in Feilding after the holiday, flung wide the door, dumped all our cases and settled to eat after the long drive, Ian challenged me with the question, 'This place is home, isn't it, Mum?' I looked at him. It was, for him. He had put down his roots. So had the other three. I replied, 'Give me a week and I'll answer you.' Right then, I couldn't. I was crying out for family, friends, something familiar, a sense of belonging, and struggling with the emptiness welling up inside.

For me our home still felt like a motel. I wanted to feel differently about it. I couldn't whip my feelings into line. I missed adult company in the house; especially after six weeks of being with other adults. Resentment choked me as I sat with four children each mealtime and longed for a more stimulating level of conversation, and for company when they all scattered to activities or homework.

I could find no corner of the house where I felt at ease. Restlessness drove me into frenzied activity that folk misjudged as healthy adjustment; signs of coping.

I woke each morning to a sinking feeling in my stomach, a breathlessness, and a desire to break out of this prison. I considered the possibility of shifting again, but my kitten poster spoke to me and I knew that moving again would solve nothing.

Yet each time I entered our street, the No Exit sign flashed at me like a neon light. I was filled with fear. Lying awake at nights, I felt dislocated. My mind filled with scenes from the manse: cosy sunny corners in the garden and the cool shady fernery smelling of damp earth and bush humus. I experienced a desperate longing to be rooted in the familiar

The Empty Tomb

and held in the arms of the one I loved. There was nothing of Garth in our new home; the train set was packed away and the boxes of books were still stored at the church. Our whole lifestyle had changed as we withdrew from the hub of church life. Instead of a ceaseless stream of people, the doorbell didn't ring, the telephone was strangely silent. The days were long and lonely while the children were at school, then erupted into extraordinary busyness when they all arrived home. No-one else was there to take a listening role, to help with homework, mend bikes, transport musical instruments to practices, attend school meetings, fix the motor mower, prune trees or cart away the rubbish.

If this was my new life, I didn't want it. I longed for the past. I could identify with the writer in Psalm 42.

> My heart breaks when I remember the past,
> when I went with the crowds to the house of God...
> Here in exile my heart is breaking...
> He has sent waves of sorrow over my soul;
> chaos roars at me like a flood.
> (Psalm 42:4, 6, 7)

Returning to church the first Sunday back in Feilding we were made so welcome, and I delighted in worship. I could not understand how I could doubt Jesus, struggle with prayer and live in such restlessness, yet still thrill to the music in worship and savour with deep hunger the words that spoke of God's faithfulness. I delighted to be with God's people and to worship. But I seemed to live in two worlds. I could not bring together the reality of Jesus I experienced in worship and the appalling absence of peace, joy and his presence I experienced for the rest of each week.

I withdrew into myself, barely reaching to my children and seldom beyond. Guilt grew as I saw how quickly I abandoned Jesus' commission, and prayer. Aneta's baby rabbits, brought home from Naseby, died in spite of all our loving care and prayers. Another young Christian leader in Feilding died suddenly. 'God,' I cried, 'where is your power? When will you answer your people's prayers? What is wrong? Are you punishing us

Shattered and Restored

for sin? Or do you grieve for us and, if so, why don't you do something?'

A Christian spoke of God's leading. I longed to be led. I was lost in a deep valley. Some folk said to me, 'You'll shift.' Some said, 'Ride it out. Make it yours and time will heal.' What was God saying? Why couldn't I hear him, see him, feel him, know him as I had in the past?

Shortly after returning to Feilding, the planning group in our parish held a lunchtime meeting and, because it was such a beautiful summer's day, the administrator chose to hold the meeting in the manse gardens. I sat with the group in the shade of spreading trees. All the familiar sounds, smells and vistas met me, overwhelmed me, and I crumpled to pieces inside. I hid my struggle from the group and bolted for home at the conclusion of the meeting, tears of grief stinging my eyes. By teatime, I had fled to my room, leaving a trail of bewildered children behind me, stormed at the Lord and then, in exhaustion, lay still.

The truth dawned. I was like Mary, crying into the empty tomb, when all the time the Lord was standing with her. Looking through her tears to where he had been, she could not see that he had moved ahead. I kept reaching back for a well-loved and safe landscape, but Jesus had moved on. Hadn't he called me last winter to come on out, to go forward? I would never find him by going backwards. He was not there anymore.

So often, the Bible speaks of God as on the move. God, in the fire and cloud, moved ahead of the Israelites. To Moses he said, 'Why are you crying out for help? Tell the people to move forward' (Exodus 14:15). In Exodus 23:20, God says, 'I will send an angel ahead of you.' The star went ahead of the wise men. The angel at the empty tomb said, 'He is going ahead of you to Galilee. There you will see him' (Matthew 28:7). I heard the Lord say to me also, 'Why are you looking backwards? I have gone ahead.' Hebrews 10:38, 39 says:

> My righteous people, however, will believe and live; but if any of them turns back, I will not be pleased with him. We are not people who turn back and are lost. Instead, we have faith and are saved.

I do not believe I turned my back on Jesus. I was looking for him, but in the past, where I had known his presence and activity. He was calling to me as he had called to Mary, drawing me away from the empty place into the place where he now was.

'Lord,' I prayed. 'Have I still not learned that the ground of my being is in you alone? Everything else has been stripped away. Finally, peace and joy have vanished as well. Yet I hear your call now, and your promise to be in this place with me.'

Right then, in my room, I made a promise to the Lord that I would settle in my new home. I would give no more thought to moving and, with his help, I would attempt to stop crying into empty tombs. I would let go the past and go forward with him, in spite of my uncertainty. While I learned this lesson at Jesus' feet, the children had cleaned up the abandoned tea things and Aneta and Katrina had prepared a beautiful card with a brightly coloured rainbow and the words: 'We still care'. They brought the card and a bowl of flowers to my room. I wept again, for joy at their love, and pain for the way I had treated them. I felt I didn't deserve such precious children. The words of an old hymn rang in my mind all week:

I have decided to follow Jesus.
No turning back.
No turning back.

It was an act of will, a decision not attended by great joy, just the realisation that forward was the only way. I had been unwilling to settle, until this point, in the land the Lord had given me. Some weeks before Christmas, I had underlined some verses from Jeremiah that seemed to have significance. The people had asked Jeremiah to pray to God to show the way they should go, and had promised 'whether it pleases us or not, we will obey the Lord our God, to whom we are asking you to pray. All will go well with us if we obey him.' Jeremiah brought this answer:

If you are *willing* to go on living in this land, then I will build you up and not tear you down; I will plant you and not pull you up...

Shattered and Restored

> Stop being afraid ... I am with you, and will rescue you...
> (Jeremiah 42:10, 11 italics mine)

The people had been unhappy with the answer. They didn't want to hear the call to live in exile and they had rebelled, bringing destruction upon themselves.

I sensed the words to settle also applied to me, but I too had sought a way out. Now, with the strong awareness that there could be no turning back, that the tomb was empty, and with the risen Lord's promise to be with me, I could say, 'I am willing, not wanting, but willing, to stop clutching my exposed roots and to put them down in this place.' With that decision came a new gratitude for my home, moments of real appreciation, and the ability to praise the Lord genuinely – not always, but at least sometimes. Two days after my decision, I received a letter from a dear friend.

> I keep thinking about Jeremiah's letter to the exiles (Jeremiah 29). The exiles kept thinking Babylon was to be a temporary home and so it was no use carrying on with life. They too had the depression that comes as a natural consequence of grieving. But Jeremiah says, 'Build houses and settle down, plant gardens and eat what they produce,' etc.
>
> In other words, 'Use your nurturing instincts through your hands and relationships. Be a good steward of all that I have given you.'
>
> It will not be easy and I urge you not to cling to the past. Let go and nurture your sons and daughters and the good earth and healing will come..
>
> I pray and send the only thing I can to help. The enclosed cheque is for you to spend on the garden...
>
> With all my love...

How wonderful is God's timing! He waited patiently for me to respond to his call, to turn from crying into an empty tomb, to be willing to make new beginnings with him. Then he sent such clear confirmation with my friend's letter and very generous gift.

God understands we will grieve for the past. He did not chastise Mary for weeping at the tomb. He called her lovingly and gently. He knew her tears blinded her vision. They blinded mine also. When looking backwards, several things happen: we lose our vision of Jesus; we see no future as we live in the past; we have no hope and no motivation; we become filled with despair and darkness. He knows all that, lovingly comes to meet us and calls us to go forward into the future which he has planned for us already.

As the hymn sung at Garth's funeral says:

Be still my soul, when dearest friends depart
And all is darkened in a vale of tears,
Then shalt thou better know His love, His heart,
Who come to soothe thy sorrow and thy fears,
Be still, my soul; thy Jesus can repay,
From His own fullness, all He takes away.

chapter
eleven

WHEN DARKNESS SEEMS FOR EVER

'Darkness and light are the same to you' (Psalm 139:12). These words from Psalm 139 baffled me. They were certainly not the same to me. Once I had lived in the light, tasted its joy and been spurred by its hope.

Depression had stalked me in the winter of 1985. But there followed the Lord's promise of restoration. Shafts of light penetrated the gloom. The Lord had shown me there could be no turning back. I had willingly agreed to go forward. Yet I slumped into deeper darkness. Why? As I let go the last strand of hope that, somehow, I could return to the life we had known, I did not stride confidently into a new future. The fact is I could not see any. With nothing to turn back to, and seemingly nothing to step forward to, I went as many do at this point – down to the bottom of the curve into depression.

It settled upon me as surely as winter. Depression is as certain in grief as joy is in loving. It sapped my energy; energy essential for climbing out of that pit. Someone once said, 'Grief is the hardest work in the world.' I believe them. It's lonely work, too. Support is essential, but grief – the inside work – is done alone and it seems to be carried out in murky blackness with very distorted vision.

During a counselling training course run in those months I was paired with a friend for an exercise in dialogue and listening. The question presented to me was, 'How do you see your future?' Through tears I sobbed, 'I don't see any future.' Around that time a page in my diary reads:

> The future looms empty, like an endless desert to trudge through in loneliness and purposelessness until age and the environment wear me down. I have a huge fear of mindless, aimless filling of time.

C.S. Lewis wrote of his experience after the death of his wife:

> And grief still feels like fear. Perhaps more strictly like suspense. Or just a waiting, just hanging about waiting for something to happen It gives life a permanently provisional feeling. It doesn't seem worth starting anything. I can't settle down. I yawn. I fidget, I smoke too much. Up till this I always had too little time. Now there is nothing but time. Almost pure time, empty successiveness.[2]

On a fine day I can see the majestic snow capped Mt Ruapehu just over one hundred kilometres away. When cloud obscures it I still know it's there. The devastating thing about depression is that when the future is obscured by grief you actually can't believe there will be one. The present lost all meaning as well, as this diary entry clearly shows:

> I'm adrift in an ocean of emptiness and anger, tossed about by every wave of emotion with no horizon in sight and no anchor. I am drowning in the storm with nothing, it seems, but my pathetic human resources. Where are you, God? Are you in the storm, the wind, or nowhere at all? I get the feeling you're trying to tell me you are the sea and if I relax I will be buoyed up. But the waves still toss me. I ride a crest, catch a view, hold my breath in wonder at your love and then promptly plummet into a trough again and am drowning in fear and blinded with the spray of defeat and confusion. When will it ever remain calm? Where is victory and power to defeat depression?

Perhaps the most lethal distortion I experienced was how I saw myself, while living that hell – as pathetic, a useless parent, unattractive and incapable of anything good. In short, there were times when I seriously considered that my children and the world would be better off without me.

Most who have lived under depression's cloud will have experienced these three things: a hopelessness about the future, a meaninglessness each day and a deep sense of worthlessness. Yet the psalmist said of God, 'Darkness and light are the same to you.' Could it be that he had clear visibility in the fog that smothered me? Did he see things differently – a different reality, more true than mine?

One day I flicked open the pages of my Bible to Song of Songs, where once, six years before, I had heard the Lord affirm me greatly. I hungered for affirmation now. I was drawn to words I had never noticed before:

> I am only a wild flower in Sharon,
> A lily in a mountain valley.
> (Song of Songs 2:1)

I felt about as obscure as a vulnerable, tiny lily in a New Zealand mountain valley, dwarfed by tall totaras and kauris, shadowed by large mamaku tree ferns and in danger of being trampled on by hikers whose eyes were on the majestic trees and lofty mountains. I felt utterly insignificant. I read on:

> Like a lily among thorns,
> is my darling among women.
> (Song of Songs 2:2)

The same image, a lily, but in a totally different setting. Here I experienced the beauty and height of the lily as it towered above a bed of tangled thistles. It was fragrant and stately, an exquisite creation bringing delight to its creator and all who saw it.

God spoke through these two short verses to affirm me – precious, valuable, a delight to his eyes. There is much said today about the need to help people develop self-esteem. I believe if it's not grounded outside self it's so much hot air and the bubble is easily burst. But when the Spirit of God affirms, it's grounded in eternal reality. It's real. Time after time God corrected my distorted view of myself with his word to me: 'You are precious and I love you' (Isaiah 43:4).

He also lifted the clouds on the future with his promises to me, beginning with the promise of restoration and repeated in other words when the fog of despair swirled around me.

> I alone know the plans I have for you, plans to bring you prosperity
> and not disaster, plans to bring about the future you hope for.
> (Jeremiah 29:11)

He sought to restore my twisted perspective of the future, the present and myself. He spoke into my darkness from his perspective in the light, rolled back the clouds a little and invited me to see the view in all its beauty and potential. He promised:

> I will lead my blind people
> by roads they have never travelled.
> I will turn their darkness into light
> and make rough country flat before them.
> These are my promises,
> and I will keep them without fail.
> (Isaiah 42:16)

I did not live those days in buoyant hope. God gave me those words as tiny seeds sown in the dark soil of hopelessness. It was months before they flowered but, meanwhile, they pointed to a reality full of hope, when I held none. Each day was still an exhausting journey but I had a choice: to believe my view and be defeated by the darkness, or to order my days on the basis of his promises. Morton Kelsey puts it this way:

When Darkness Seems For Ever

Step out in hope, keeping an eye peeled for experiences that reveal the victory and the guidance of this other realm. This is not a matter of faith. Faith is a gift that comes, the gift of assurance that the powers of light have conquered and will keep on defeating the powers of darkness. Hope on the other hand is our attitude of looking steadfastly towards that victory and trying to order our lives towards it.[3]

To order my life towards that victory required an act of will in two major areas: my *actions* and my *attitudes*.

While depressed, I had no desire to get up, to cook meals or to clean house. I lacked motivation to visit people, read books, sing or play. Everything required too much effort. The battle was on between my will and my emotions.

Still I chose to get up each day when it was much easier to pull the covers back over and blot out reality. I chose to clean the house when I couldn't care less. Neglecting it resulted in deeper depression. Many mornings and evenings I went for a walk and during the day I gardened. I believe physical exercise is one of God's antidotes for depression. On black days I couldn't care if I never ate, but I also believe a balanced diet affects emotional and spiritual well-being, so I marshalled my flagging energy to prepare good food for us. I deliberately reduced my consumption of tea and coffee which compound depression. In short, what I was doing was seeking to co-operate with God in the promise he had made to me – that I would be whole again – by willing to act in ways that facilitated that healing.

I have never been one to pamper myself, yet there were times when the most helpful thing I could do to reinforce God's word that I was special was to enjoy a bubble bath, find a friend to go to the pictures with or treat myself in some way. Anticipating a treat helped me survive the tasteless days. Ian lived from one camp to the next. Setting his sights on those special times helped him trudge through the dark days between.

The mind is exceptionally vulnerable in one depressed. I found a daily dose of news with its negative items and disasters plunged me into deeper despair. So I turned to books that offered hope and listened to music

111

offering praise to God. I watched TV comedies, or nature programmes which increased my appreciation and wonder at God's creativity. It was important to feed my mind on positive things.

I had most difficulty with ordering my attitudes towards that victory. Maintaining a grateful attitude can be hard work when all joy is dusty memory. I knew gratitude was a sure cure for depression and self-pity, the special illness at the heart of all grief, but it didn't come easily.

I recall a morning when I gazed out the kitchen window at the wintry scene and thought moodily, 'What is there to thank you for, God?' The rain dribbled down the window, the paths were awash, the air cold, the fire barely warming the chill room. My gaze settled on the bright yellow lemons reaching maturity on the bush by the back door. Deliberately I thanked God for the splash of colour in a dreary landscape. My thanks felt as sour as the new lemons; praise issuing from a barren heart. Yet it was the best response I could offer. I believe God was pleased with my faithfulness more than my fruitfulness at that time. He knew an uprooted plant couldn't bear fruit. But if rooted in him, one day my praise would again spring from a truly glad heart.

I frequently called to mind past activity of God in our family, remembering how he had led us, healed our memories, met our needs. Often it was easier to look back and see where he had been than to see how he was with me in the present struggle.

The writer of Psalm 77 understood well the inability to see God in depression:

> All night long I lift my hands in prayer,
> but I cannot find comfort.
> When I think of God, I sigh;
> when I meditate, I feel discouraged.

He questioned whether God was still present and active:

> Has he stopped loving us?
> Does his promise no longer stand?

Then to restore his faith he, too, remembered the past:

> I will recall the wonder you did in the past.
> I will think about all you have done;
> I will meditate on all your mighty acts.

Many psalms I discovered in this time move from a cry of anguish to a song of praise. Reading Psalm 22 one day, what unfolded before me was a progressive pattern from despair to confident hope. The beauty of this psalm and others like it was that it began where I was and I felt an instant affinity.

> My God, my God, why have you abandoned me?
> I have cried desperately for help,
> but still it does not come.

No pretence here, stark reality, and I knew his cry. It was mine also. But the psalm drew me out of the bleak present moment with reminders of God's activity.

> It was you who brought me safely through birth...

Pleas for his intervention echoed mine:

> O Lord, don't stay away from me!

The psalm drew me from self-awareness to God awareness, and from pity to praise...

> I will tell my people what you have done;
> I will praise you in their assembly...

I was drawn from individuality into the concept of community with its sense of belonging.

> In the whole assembly I will praise you…
> In the presence of those who worship you.

The movement of the psalm is *outward*:

> All nations will remember the Lord.
> All races will worship him.

upward:

> The Lord is king…

forward:

> Future generations will serve him…
> People not yet born will be told…

and from *negative to positive*:

> The Lord saved his people.

In thirty-one verses the psalmist's whole attitude and outlook ha changed. He was doing what Kelsey speaks of: 'trying to order our live towards that victory'. That required right thinking and discipline. I foun it so easy to fall into a pit of despair; so difficult to climb out again.

One day when heaviness filled my heart and bones I sought relief i gardening. With each spadeful of soil turned I vented my feelings to Goc 'If Garth were here, God, I wouldn't have to do this heavy work alone nor would I be parenting alone. Without his love I fail my children. Goc can't you see I can't manage without Garth? I hurt the children so muc because of my pain and then guilt crushes my spirit.'

As the heavy clay soil spilled off the spade I continued to spill my feeling to God. 'Have you seen the children's pain? How can they be stable withou a dad? Who can these growing children turn to for a male role model?'

A car pulled up the drive. A young female friend got out and her weary expression caught my attention. 'What's wrong? Are you okay?'

She was not. Over a cup of coffee she poured out her pent up frustration with her husband. She was sure he was ruining her life and she would be better off without him. Before we'd even finished coffee a teenager called and, slumping in a chair, she began to pour out the anger she felt towards her father. She was convinced he was wrecking her life.

I had spent all afternoon blaming my problems on the loss of a husband, and my children's problems on the absence of a father, and here before me were two people equally convinced that husbands and fathers were their major problems. Suddenly I understood that the answer lay not in a change of situation but in a change of response. There are seldom good reasons for suffering but there can be good responses.

God kept pointing me in the direction of praise and gratitude when I least felt like responding that way. My attempts to maintain a positive attitude of praise were sorely tested at times.

On one occasion I left the laundry tub to fill while attending to another task and returned much later to meet a lake lapping at the door. The hall carpet was awash with hot water. It had to be lifted, dried and re-laid. For days we padded down a concrete hall while the carpet dried outside draped over garden furniture and boxes. Embarrassment cancelled praise.

On another occasion, when we had finally furnished the attic for Ian, Jim was assisting me in transferring my furniture into the larger bedroom. I was really looking forward to the space and feeling very positive. Then we inadvertently undid the wrong bolts on my bed and, with a sickening twang, the wire-wove curled itself up, bending the bolts in its bid for freedom. My first response was far from praising the Lord. My bed was distorted grotesquely and looked beyond repair. Swallowing what little was left of my pride I called a friend and, with the help of a car jack, the wire-wove was finally restored to its correct position, but not without a struggle. The thing definitely had a will of its own. Much later we could laugh about the whole ridiculous situation but at the time I was frustrated and humiliated. Many tasks left me feeling my inadequacy and ignorance. At such times praise escaped me.

Anxiety also sapped my ability to praise. As their only parent, I felt extremely responsible for my children. Traumas affecting them weighed heavily on me. Ian was delivered home one day from the cycle race track white and shaken, with shredded clothing and skin, having come off a bike at speed denting a fence pole with his head – fortunately encased in a crash helmet.

All these situations gave me an understanding of what the Bible means when it refers to a sacrifice of praise. It's costly. Self-pity, frustration and anxiety had to be sacrificed in a deliberate attempt to be grateful for God's keeping.

Oh the relief on the days when God himself put a song in my heart. The day our cat gave birth to four little white and stripy kittens in the dark warmth of the attic, we climbed up to rejoice in the new life and watch the proud mother. The day I first heard a fantail's distinct call and watched it flit about the pear tree, catching insects in mid-flight, and the morning I heard the little grey warbler sing his unfinished symphony from the top of the gum tree, my heart was genuinely glad. Just as the grey warbler's song was unfinished so also was my grief. Sometimes my heart could sing, sometimes the song choked in my throat. The Bible says:

A cheerful heart is a good medicine,
but a downcast spirit dries up the bones.
(Proverbs 17:22 RSV)

How true. My spirit was downcast on many occasions. The result was as the Bible predicted. My shoulders developed a continual throb, making some tasks painful and others impossible. Physiotherapy offered only partial relief. I knew stress was the cause. I seemed powerless to change that. The more I ached, the more stressful I became, because I couldn't do the tasks required of me. The winter of 1986 dragged on interminably. It was exceptionally wet, and the sunshine rarely broke through the blanket of grey cloud. Precious plants transplanted from the manse gave up the struggle in the heavy soil and died. Some hung on by a thread, a shadow of their former glory, struggling with clay and poor drainage.

I visited a friend one day and, sweeping her arm around her study, she confessed, 'This shambles is a reflection of me. I need to bring order to both.' Spontaneously I replied, 'My garden is a perfect reflection of me. Sour, cold and in need of draining.'

My feeble attempts to praise God were swamped by the bitterness that was settling in my heart. How I resented the new responsibility, the endless tasks associated with a shift of home, the loneliness of solo parenting, the lack of companionship. I snapped at the children. I was easily irritated by their demands, even legitimate ones. Nothing held any joy.

I woke one morning with a snippet of a dream clearly in my mind. In the dream I was cooking and had included vinegar instead of oil in the recipe. The confusion had arisen because they were in identical containers. The meal was unpalatable. I suspected that I was the vessel and that the bitterness that flowed from me was making family life as sour as vinegar. The oil of blessing and healing was needed to restore harmony.

The message was reinforced twice that week as the Lord drew my attention to two verses in Scripture:

Do not overcome evil by evil, but overcome evil with good.
(Romans 12:21 RSV)

Guard against turning back from the grace of God. Let no one become like a bitter plant that grows up and causes many troubles with its poison. (Hebrews 12:15)

'Lord,' I asked, 'how do I drain off the bitterness? How do I change vinegar for the oil of healing? Your healing peace and grace can't flow into my bitter heart. It's clogged like my garden.'

Bitterness is entirely foreign to God's purpose for wholeness in our lives and, in fact, it prevents us from discovering God's purpose. Psalm 73 says:

When my thoughts were bitter
and my feelings were hurt,

> I was as stupid as an animal;
> I did not understand you.
> (Psalm 73:21, 22)

When I flick through the pages of my diary written that bleak winter, I find one recurring phrase: 'I can't'.

> I am empty of love and full of pain. To empty the pain feels like trying to tip out a huge drum full of fluid while standing inside. *I can't.*

> There has to be a key to unlock your limitless resources, making connections with you that bring peace and not pain, healing and not hopelessness, love in the place of loneliness. But *I can't* find the key.

> *I can't* get away from myself and what is inside. If I stop rushing, it overwhelms me and I am crushed. Yet when I fill each moment with frenzied activity, *I can't* keep my focus on you, Lord.

> I yearn for Garth's love and companionship. I feel starved to the point where I have nothing to give my children. You, Lord, are 'love' but I can't tap that huge reservoir. In my pain I block it.

It looks depressing. It was depressing. Yet woven through those statements is another theme: 'I want to'. There was the desire to: drain the bitterness; find connection with God's resource; focus on Jesus; be filled with his love.

'Looking steadfastly towards that victory'. Though I failed often to order my life towards it, God saw the desire and was glad. He did not chide me for the failures. In this instant age, God often remains the only one who recognises that the path to wholeness is a process.

I wanted God to zap me so it would all be better in an instant. I was tired of waking to a sick feeling in my stomach and dragging myself through tasteless daily routines. I longed for an end to the struggle to hang on to God's promises. I wanted to see them fulfilled now, blossoming into reality. The days when the promises seemed empty I felt as a little seed buried six feet underground, wondering if I would ever grow to experience the light and warmth again.

I believe God saw the struggle for meaning as I poured myself into house and garden. He wept for the disillusionment as it all tasted bitter. I know now he ached for the pain I inflicted on my children and they on me, and rejoiced when we could embrace and say, 'Sorry'.

I believe his heart rejoiced in my faltering attempts to co-operate with him in these four directions:

1. Towards self – to take care of diet, rest, exercise, play.
2. Towards the world – to be grateful for my home, health, children, friends, sunshine, flowers, birds.
3. Towards God – to praise him and to take him at his word when it seemed empty and so long in being realised.
4. Towards others – to listen, to love, to care and to seek forgiveness when I failed.

Each choice I made to order my life towards his promises brought tiny changes inside. A lot happens in the darkness. A buried seed striving to reach the light changes, breaking its protective case, reaching for where it knows life is to be found. Likewise in my darkness, a movement took place, imperceptible to me then, from the resistance of 'I won't accept what has been dealt me', through the frustration of 'I can't change anything', to the birth of the desire, 'I want to seek life again'.

My darkness was not dark to him. He would complete what he had begun. He would draw me out of my darkness and into his marvellous light. Meanwhile he held me under the shadow of his wings – safety in a dark place.

chapter

twelve

IN TWO MINDS

Hebrews 12:13 caught my attention one day: 'Keep walking on straight paths, so that the lame foot may not be disabled, but instead be healed.' Which paths were straight? Which would lead to healing? Which intensify my crippled state?

I dreamt one night that I stood undecided before two paths. One was a smooth broad highway to the top of the mountain, but the sweet taste of success on reaching the summit turned to the bitter realisation that I was trapped in beauty devoid of soul, like candyfloss at the fun fair. The other path wound its way downhill through tall bush and tangled undergrowth, then gradually ascended, twisting, narrow and treacherous, to arrive at the summit. That difficult path provided, in time, deep satisfaction and healing. But on waking I was still unable to decide which real life situation was related to which path.

I had faced such questions for months. Trusting Jesus led to life. But what did it mean to trust Jesus in a specific situation? Months before, while trying to choose a house, I questioned, 'Does trust mean waiting for a house that has all we need or does it mean letting go of our conditions, knowing Christ is all we need?' The Bible says the peace that Christ gives is to guide us in the decisions we make (Colossians 3:15).

Did that mean waiting for a sense of peace before making a move or did it mean moving, believing that God would affirm our trust with his peace as he did to Abraham.

I wrestled with the age-old question of how to walk in the will of God in a physical world requiring practical decisions. If only I had the mind of Christ I would see more clearly. But often I was in two minds. Have you ever been in two minds about anything? The human mind has an amazing ability to hold two completely opposing views at the same time. I had held trust and unbelief in tension all year.

On the one hand I could proclaim, 'I love you, God. I trust you. I know you love me and will never let me down. I believe you care about our choice of house.' But with the next breath I could think, 'God, you let Garth die. I'm angry and can't trust you any more. You abandoned us in our deepest need. Do you really care about what house we live in?'

I'm not unique in holding such opposites in tension. A glance at the Psalms will reveal similar contrasting views only verses apart. Psalm 22:1, 2 expresses doubt:

> My God, my God, why have you abandoned me?
> I have cried desperately for help, but still it does not come.
> During the day I call to you, my God, but you do not answer…

Yet verses 24 and 25 declare triumphantly:

> He does not neglect the poor or
> ignore their suffering;
> he does not turn away from them,
> but answers when they call for help.
> In the full assembly I will praise you
> for what you have done.

Psalm 44:4, 5, 8 is positive:

> You give victory to your people,

and by your power we defeat our enemies.
We will always praise you
and give thanks to you for ever.

But verse 9 says, in contrast:

But now you have rejected us and let us be defeated;
you no longer march out with our armies.

How can two such opposing views be held in the one mind? I believe it happens when we experience two distinct realities in conflict – *emotional reality* and *spiritual truth.*

On one occasion, when waves of depression threatened to obscure my view of God, I recalled the pictures I had focused on in the hospital ward when Garth's illness was first diagnosed. I re-entered each scene in imagination. On the cliff above the sea I slipped, tumbling past rocks and bushes, grasping in vain for something to break my fall. Suddenly the Lord reached out, stopped my fall and set me on my feet beside him. In the river scene I was being swept downstream towards powerful rapids. I panicked until I saw the Lord standing waist deep, steady as a rock in the rapids, his eye on me, his arms outstretched to catch me. In all four scenes I was falling, drowning, sliding or lost, portraying clearly the reality of my emotional state. Yet in each scene the Lord was in complete control, determined to rescue me. Both the emotional and spiritual truths were powerfully real.

When I focused on my feelings I knew I couldn't survive. When I focused on Christ I knew he would re-establish me. The trouble was that in the turbulence of the moment sustained focus was lost and I was tossed between the two realities – a widening chasm between facts and feelings. They seemed irreconcilable.

I knew I had a lovely home and wonderful children. I also knew deep restlessness and ingratitude. I knew God stood by me, yet I also felt utter loneliness. I knew the fact of God's faithfulness, yet I experienced feelings of hopelessness. Both were equally real.

Shattered and Restored

How then to handle the conflict? 'Pull yourself together' is the most frequently heard advice to those experiencing this dilemma. So they try, and find the division so great they can't do it. They may deny or abandon either the facts or the feelings as untrue in an attempt to solve the pull within. But denial is dangerous and ultimately no solution.

Emotions, when denied, settle into the subconscious and affect our physical and spiritual health, breaking out in ulcers, rheumatism, cancer, depression, insomnia, etc. When we fail to own our emotions then they own us. They become powerful, destructive forces. Often in shame and confusion we bury our strong feelings, especially when they appear to conflict with the spiritual truth we have learned. Well meaning but misguided Christians don't help either when they try to dispel our confusion, yet will not listen or accept our feelings as real and powerful forces.

Jesus didn't deny his emotions. He cried, 'My God, my God, why did you abandon me?' (Matthew 27:46). He felt abandoned. He owned his feelings and expressed them to God. But he didn't deny God either. He went right on to own the fact that God would never abandon him. Immediately after expressing his feeling of abandonment he said, 'Father! In your hands I place my spirit' (Luke 23:46), acknowledging a fact in direct opposition to his feelings at that moment of pain.

The answer is not to submerge feelings, but to submit them openly to Christ. Owning feelings doesn't mean accepting them as the whole truth, but it does mean recognising their reality, declaring that to Jesus and, in the light of his reality, the whole truth will finally emerge.

For weeks I would attend worship and receive the truth of God's love and grace and be encouraged by the songs of praise. I would hungrily grasp spiritual truth in the readings and sermon, and my shattered picture of God would begin to reform. Then I would walk out of worship into loneliness and emptiness. The combined anger of five hurting people and the emotional reality of grief would stand in stark contrast to the truth I perceived in worship.

I tried in vain to reassemble my picture of God. There were new pieces that wouldn't fit. The rich gold of God's Word clashed with the darker pieces of my grief. The shapes wouldn't fit either. There were comfortable pieces of truth I had held and worn smooth through the years which would not interlock with the jagged new pieces of pain.

At times, in order to hold onto the Word of life, I tried to deny the painful reality of anger and loneliness. At other times, when emotion ran strong, I responded by denying God's Word because it seemed so false in the light of my feelings.

What was I to do? It was at that time that I stumbled upon this concept of twin realities in conflict and how important it is to own it *all* and bring *all* to the light of Christ for reconciliation. I saw how the Psalmist did it:

> My heart breaks when I remember the past,
> Why am I so sad?
> Why am I so troubled?
> (Psalm 42:4, 5)

He owned it all, yet went on to say,

> I will put my hope in God,
> and once again I will praise him,
> my saviour and my God.
> (Psalm 42:5b)

I realised the need to acknowledge the brokenness, but also the need to submit it to God. Both those who submerge their feelings and those who cling to them like a child's 'cuddly' will self-destruct. We own our feelings in order to bring them to the healing light of Christ to be transformed. The Psalmist wrote:

> As a deer longs for a stream of cool water,
> so I long for you, O God.
> (Psalm 42:1)

Shattered and Restored

In January I wrote:

> I long to love you, yet my heart is broken
> And love can't flow from the shattered pieces.
> So I come and place the shattered pieces in your hands
> For you to touch, to heal and make whole again
> That I may love you with a strong and vibrant love,
> Pulsating through a mended heart.

Submission doesn't come naturally to the human race and, like Adam of old, we try to cover up that of which we are ashamed. If that fails, we may try to whip our feelings into line ourselves. It is a commonly held Christian teaching that if we receive the truth of God's Word into our minds, then our corrected thought patterns will tow our wayward feelings into line. There is one basic error in that theory. It is a self-help system allowing Christ access to our minds only while we, in presumption, seek by sheer willpower to rectify our emotional imbalance. It's not willpower we need but Christ's transforming power. A statement in *The Other Side of Silence* by Morton Kelsey, was like a laser beam of light, cutting me free from the prison of past theology:

> Catholic and protestant thought is rooted in the scholastic reverence for mind alone. Human beings can be viewed as essentially rational beings. In this belief, if one brings the mind to the right point of view, then the rest of the human being will come around, including our emotions and our behaviour which is largely influenced by emotions. Unfortunately this is simply not true.[4]

For six months I had certainly discovered it to be not true. I could not, by myself, make my feelings fall into line with the spiritual truth. Quite the reverse. Powerful emotions threatened to destroy my once vibrant faith. The truth finally dawned. Christ needed to touch and transform each aspect of my being directly and not be restricted to working through my mind alone.

The next question was how to let Christ have access to my emotions. Deep, meaningful worship, the powerful sacrament of communion and songs of praise opened my heart for Jesus to touch the seat of my emotions. Jesus said worship was to be in spirit as well as in truth. When I worshipped with my heart and feelings as well as my mind, then God brought the oil of healing to my wounded spirit laid open to his ministry. Sometimes I wept in worship – tears of anger and frustration, tears of pain and loss. Those times he touched my heart. At times I rejoiced in his love and he seemed to rejoice with me till I felt my heart would burst.

In dreams and through reliving Bible passages, as I had done with the beach scene and Lazarus, Jesus gained access to my submerged feelings. Inner healing also allowed him to touch and transform emotions directly. I learned not to fear strong feelings, but to allow them to surface fully, alive and kicking into the presence of Christ, and I discovered that, as Christ poured the oil of his healing on my feelings, my doubts about him also calmed. I cannot undervalue the power of the mind submitted to Christ, but I know now that all of me must be submitted to him, then he can bring his mighty power to transform emotions, spirit and mind. He alone can bring the twin realities into one, reconciling my two minds into one, setting me free.

So I brought my raw emotions, ugly as they were, to Jesus, told him how I felt and submitted myself to his transforming touch. At the same time, I sought to reinforce the spiritual foundation left unstable by the pounding waves of my emotions.

On one occasion, when I felt God to be so impotent, indifferent, remote and uncaring, I deliberately headed up a page in my diary, 'The God I Knew', and listed the attributes I had believed so firmly in the past and had held as undeniable truth. These things I wrote:

The God I Knew

1. Loves me with an unchanging, passionate love.
2. Is amazingly creative. The whole world is a work of art proclaiming his creativity.

3. Is a perfectionist; a master of detail. The fine anatomy of the tiniest creature and the workings of a human ear or eye are without equal.
4. Is pro-life. Growth and life characterise his world. Life springs up in deserts and barren volcanic areas. Blades of grass thrust through concrete jungles.
5. Constantly restores. Broken skin heals. Broken bones mend. Scarred landscapes are reclothed.
6. Brings harmony in place of discord.
7. Unifies and co-ordinates. He majors on integration, not disintegration.
8. Is all positive. Where God is, there is hope, faith, trust, love, peace, acceptance, gratitude, praise, forgiveness, goodness and mercy. Where God is, positive attitudes rule, facilitating harmony and integration.
9. Brings freedom. His love does not possess or consume. His love releases people and gives them freedom to choose.
10. Is truth.
11. The God I knew was powerful.

As I rebuilt my concept of God, the realisation grew that God is not a concept, but a companion, that truth is not a formula, but a friend. And friendships and companionships change and grow. They develop as the personalities interact. I can no longer put a tidy frame around my carefully constructed picture of God and hang it for future reference. Instead I can only put my hand in his, walk through all the landscapes of life with him and discover more about him as we journey.

I had already discovered that God cared about my feelings and that he had the power to calm them. When in two minds my life had been characterised by confusion and deep fear. He looked upon my fear with love and drew me toward himself. The Bible records many instances where God drew his people out of fear by his love. To Joshua God said, 'Do not be afraid. I will be with you.' Mary and Joseph were afraid, but God didn't look for another set of parents for Jesus. The shepherds were afraid. The angels sang to them. Peter feared the water. Jesus didn't leave him to drown; he reached out and lifted him. It is open rebellion, not fear, that alienates us from God. Saul kept the sheep, but lost the Holy Spirit. Ananias and Sapphira lied and God took their lives.

At one point of time when I prayed to God about my shaky walk with him and told him my doubts and fears, I saw a picture of myself teetering precariously on a narrow plank above a great gaping hole. Jesus called to me to come to him across the plank. Several realities presented themselves. The hole was very real. It represented the loss of Garth. My fear and instability were real. Jesus' invitation was equally real. On my plank I had several options:

(a) I could stand frozen, looking into the hole until I fell into depression.
(b) I could step off the plank and run back to a familiar landscape – only God had moved on and the past was empty.
(c) I could try by my efforts to fill the hole with the things of this world and avoid walking the plank, but I would lose sight of Jesus.
(d) I could look up to Jesus and take one small step at a time, believing in the strength of the plank – the foundation Jesus laid before life's explosion left the gaping wound in my spirit.

The two steps to reconciling my double-mindedness were, firstly, to acknowledge the hole (emotional truth) and, secondly, to trust as I moved across the plank to Jesus (spiritual truth).

For a while on holiday I sat on my plank swinging my legs until God spoke to me in the hills and the clear dam and the rainbow. Then with his promise to restore etched on my spirit, I could inch my way along the plank, my eyes on him for stability. My slow progress was not lack of faith, as some may have judged it. It's always faith to step to Jesus, no matter how small the step.

Zacchaeus climbed a tree.
Matthew came from behind a desk.
A soldier came three miles.

Shattered and Restored

> A woman stretched out her hand.
> Peter came on the water,
> but Mary could only stand in deep longing.
> Jesus knew her heart and he came to her.
> He came to Peter fishing in disillusionment.
> He came to Thomas locked in doubt.
> He came to Peter drowning in disbelief
> and he came to me in that place of emptiness and longing.

He still comes to us, especially when we are most unable to move ourselves. He came right to the tomb to free Lazarus. 'The Lord is near to those who are discouraged' (Psalm 34:18a). When we think he has abandoned us completely then he is nearest. Our feelings may not say so, but it's true.

On the cross Jesus cried, 'Why did you abandon me?' Yet God was in it all – in the darkest hour, convicting the soldier, rending the temple curtain, controlling the weather and providing the ultimate answer for you and me in the power of the cross and in the gift of new life in him.

There came a time when Peter was in two minds about Jesus. He had a body of spiritual truth, well established through first-hand experience of living with Jesus. His own mother-in-law had been healed. He had experienced Jesus' powerful preaching and healing. He had exercised the power to heal and cast out demons. Yet the day came when his feelings of fear and confusion left him in two minds about Jesus. Jesus foresaw it long before Peter experienced the conflict and, while Peter still felt comfortable and unruffled Jesus warned him of the new landscape he was about to enter; the testing he would go through. Jesus did not say to Peter, 'When it happens, pull yourself together.' Nor did he say, 'Hang onto the Word of God. Don't believe your feelings. They lie.' No. Instead he said, 'But I have prayed for you, Simon, that your faith fail not. And when you turn back to me, you must strengthen your brothers.'

While I battled the conflict within, Jesus prayed for me also, 'that my faith fail not,' and he was confident. He did not say, '*If* you turn back to me', he said, '*when*'. He knew it was only a matter of time before the two realities could come together and in the meantime in answer to my desperate question, 'What is truth?' he responded, 'I am the truth.' In John from chapter 5 to chapter 20 Jesus says, 'I am telling you the truth,' twenty-three times.

He laid before me a summary of the movement needed to bring together facts and feelings. It's found in Hebrews. The direction is towards God. The call is for honesty:

So let us come near to God with a sincere heart... (10:22).

Spiritual reality is rooted in God's promise, not feelings:

Let us hold on firmly to the hope ... because we can trust God to keep his promise. (10:23)

Wait and recognise that God promises to restore:

You need to be patient in order to do the will of God and receive what he promises. (10:36)

The movement is forward:

We are not people who turn back and are lost. Instead we have faith and are saved. (10:39)

God recognises our emotions will blind us to the truth:

To have faith is '...to be certain of the things we cannot see'. (11:1)

The discouragement of overwhelming emotions can cause unbelief. Therefore the need to focus on Jesus:

So then let us rid ourselves ... of the sin that holds on to us so tightly ...Let us keep our eyes fixed on Jesus. (12:1, 2)

God calls for steady progress on a faith plank:

> Keep walking on straight paths. (12:13)

When you can't feel your faith, or feel good, or feel God, the truth is he's real and his kingdom is unshakeable:

> You have not come, as the people of Israel came, to what you can feel …You have come to Jesus, who arranged the new covenant … Let us be thankful, then, because we receive a kingdom that cannot be shaken. (12:18, 24, 28)

God will provide. God will heal. God will get the glory:

> May the God of peace provide you with every good thing you need in order to do his will, and may he, through Jesus Christ, do in us what pleases him. And to Christ be the glory for ever and ever! (13:20–21)

The verse that first captured my attention: 'Keep walking on straight paths…' (Hebrews 12:13b) began to make sense. I had been on a zigzag track moving to and fro between faith and feelings. Jesus invited me to bring the zigs and the zags, the conflict of my two minds, to him and allow him to set me on a straight path to healing.

There is a song from the sixties with the title: 'Give it all to Jesus'. I gave it all – my two minds, my solid foundation of facts and my shaky feelings. I watched him transform it all into one solid truth, one path to the summit. I am the recipient of his unifying love.

chapter

thirteen

GIVE ME YOUR CLOAK

Me – lost for words? I'd tried many times to write this chapter, each time returning to square one, empty of any approach and saturated with coffee. I put it aside for weeks on end, returning to it with the feeling evoked by a plate of cold porridge.

Finally, I shared my frustration with Jesus. After all he was the one who wrote it all so clearly into my life in the first place. So I wrote it all back to him as a gift. We reflected together all day and I lived again the wonder of his graciousness as I talked to him on the end of my pen.

As dusk sealed the day he spoke to me. 'Elsa, are you willing to share this conversation with your readers?'

That's scary. I have a poster whose words express how my heart was feeling: 'Fragile – please handle with prayer'.

Lord, I don't know how to write this chapter. You know I've tried all year and filled the rubbish tin with countless aborted attempts. It isn't that I don't know what I want to say; you brought a pulsating reality to birth within me. So what's the problem, Lord?

I think I'm afraid, Lord, afraid of stomping all over people's wounded spirits with the hobnails of my clumsiness. I know only one who can handle this topic with the gentleness, yet firmness, it requires and that's you. I have only to look back to the way you directed me, to know that no-one else could have led me there as you did. When I think about it, it was a clever bit of work, Lord, because I was still looking sideways at you, unsure of the degree of trust to place in you. Yet you saw a spark of trust, a measure of love and you matched it with your huge love and drew me on.

Do you remember those frenzied restless days in 1986 when I tried so hard to be positive and active, only I couldn't fool you about what was inside?

Lord, I remember one of those days so well. The sofa bathed in sunlight beckoned invitingly. I curled up to rest a moment from housework. The sun's rays cast a golden glow and the warmth seeped into my weary body. A sentence drifted into my mind as I lingered there: 'Be a lizard, bask in the sun.' Strange! I wasn't thinking about lizards. I was feeling guilty about unfinished tasks. But the words persisted. I let my thoughts drift back to childhood days spent sitting on piles of sun-drenched rocks watching the native lizards lying so still absorbing the sun's rays through their sleek skins till warmed and energised they darted off in search of a tasty morsel.

They were your words, Lord. 'Be a lizard, bask in the sun.' They were in sharp contrast to my inner voice demanding performance and heaping condemnation. I recognised your voice, Lord, and I nestled in that sunny corner a while and let you love me, filling my cold and sluggish spirit with your warmth. For a moment I tasted peace and, Lord, it was such a rare experience that year.

I believe now it's not because you were unwilling to give but because I was often unable to receive.

I really hungered for the reality of Psalm 131:2.

I am content and at peace.
As a child lies quietly in its mother's arms,
so my heart is quiet within me.

But I knew and you knew that mostly my heart was anything but quiet. Lord, you knew I was doing all I could to climb out of depression. It was you who showed me how to nourish myself, how to feed my mind, how to offer praise even as a sacrifice when it felt hollow and you were wonderfully drawing into harmony emotional and spiritual truth. But something was still missing. Lord, I felt something held me captive and, for once, I wasn't actually blaming you.

Psalm 107 caught my attention one day. It looked like me.

> Some were living in gloom and darkness,
> prisoners suffering in chains...

Why?

> Because they had rebelled against
> the commands of Almighty God...

I didn't like that bit. I didn't think I was rebelling. Quite the reverse. Wasn't I really trying?

> They were worn out from hard work

That sounded like me, Lord. The psalm went on to say you would rescue when I called. Well, wasn't that what I had been doing for months, Lord? Why the delay?

One word seemed to surface often in those days, Lord. *Acceptance.* I suppose I knew it was the turning point. Garth used to call it the key back to wholeness – acceptance. But he wasn't around to tell me how to turn it. My efforts must have looked so ridiculous to you, Lord; as stupid as a person whose efforts to sleep drive away the very thing he desires.

You pictured acceptance for me in that tiny snippet of a dream where I was stomping about the lawn and suddenly a daisy emerged at my feet and turned its simple open face to the sun. In my dream I paused to admire it, conscious that I had nearly stomped it to death. I heard your words clearly, Lord. 'Acceptance will come as easily as that daisy. Suddenly it will be there. Relax. Your striving will only endanger it.'

All very well for you to say, Lord. I found a kindred restless spirit in C. S. Lewis after his wife died.

> The time when there is nothing at all in your soul except a cry for help may be just the time God can't give it. You are like a drowning man who can't be helped because he clutches and grabs. Perhaps your own reiterated cries deafen you to the voice you hoped to hear.[5]

Knowing I was not alone, Lord, cheered a little but solved nothing really. The storm still raged inside. Then you gave me this new insight that at the centre of the hurricane is a calm spot. You told me you were in that calm spot and I recorded these words in my diary: 'The key is not to try to outrun the storm but to hug its centre.'

You kept turning me from an attitude of self-preservation to one of seeking your provision; a very biblical approach which is what I'd expect from you. When I look back on the messages you managed to sneak through my noisy barrage they were quite unique:

Be a lizard, bask in the sun.
Wait for the daisy gently. Don't kill it.
Hug the eye of the storm.

They were graphic pictures and briefly they quietened me. But Lord, when my anxious heart beat a little less noisily other sounds emerged from the depths – a disturbing cacophony: sighs of resentment, the roar of anger, the shudder of fear and a twang of guilt. Lord, I really didn't want to own that noise as issuing from me, and I hoped you hadn't heard it. How foolish! Of course you had. I tried excusing it as the loss I had sustained. You acknowledged that the wounds to my spirit were real and you reminded me that you were bathing them and had your heart set to heal them. But what you showed me, as well, is that deep wounds are vulnerable to contamination. They are breeding grounds for very unsavoury guests. Anger, resentment, self-pity and fear had muddied your reflection in my life and stained the river of the Holy Spirit so that what

Give Me Your Cloak

often issued from me was not sweet, clear and refreshing, but undrinkable and bitter. My children knew that only too well and so did you, Lord.

I marvel at the gentle distinction you made as you helped me face the contamination. You never once called grief a sin. You made a distinction between sin and the emotional wound that caused it. You showed me that you bind and heal emotional wounds with deep compassion. But then you gently pointed out that you can't treat destructive attitudes that find entry through those wounds the same way. There was no point in bathing them. They needed eviction notices and since the house they resided in was mine, it rested with me to tell them they were not welcome. Lord, right then I caught an uncomfortable glimpse of the wounds I was inflicting on your Holy Spirit as you tried to bandage mine.

You weren't the only one to tell me what was happening in my life. Only I didn't receive it too well from other people, even when I asked them for help because I knew I was in a prison.

John, your servant minister, in his honesty, told me I was stubborn. I really didn't like that label. So I checked it out with you. I should have known I'd get the truth. Do you remember what you said? I do.

> I invited you to bask like a lizard, but you writhe like an octopus. I showed you to wait for the flower of acceptance. You trample all over it trying to force growth. I invited you to hug the centre of the storm and you battle against the wind of my spirit, exhausted and discouraged. That's stubborn.

By this time, Lord, I knew resentment and its cousin, anger, were major blocks to my healing, but I seemed unable to dislodge them. Surely if I didn't want them they should just go? Lord, you watched me run in circles like a dog trying to catch its tail, getting nowhere. I called on your servant, Margaret, during that time and she asked me what I thought was a very strange question. It wasn't strange to you. I'm pretty sure you prompted her to ask it. 'What's the spin-off of staying angry?' she asked.

I had no answer for her. I thought I wanted to be rid of it. That's why I'd gone to her for help. I remember carrying that question home and spreading it out before you. Your explanation: 'Human support is the spin-off. You fear self-sufficiency, even my sufficiency, in case you lose the human companionship, which you hunger for.'

Suddenly, I understood your strange question to the cripple at the pool, 'Do you want to get well?' (John 5:6). Getting well can be scary and fear may drown the very drive for freedom. Letting go costs.

Lord, all I seemed to have done those two years was let go. First Garth, then a host of related things. My dignity and pride had long since gone. Many good things I'd had to let go and you were calling me to let go a whole new bundle of things – mostly bad and destructive attitudes.

That ought to be easy. But there was a catch. To let go all resentment and anger meant saying it was okay to be in this new home I didn't like with this new lifestyle I detested. In short, Lord, it meant acceptance. There was that word again, Lord. Was acceptance to be found not by stomping it into existence but by letting go? Was that what you meant by those pictures of lizards, daisies and storms?

Lord, you know my brain worked overtime to find a solution satisfactory to me. I wanted to be out of the prison and free, but I was at that time not willing to accept what had been dealt me, or to trust you in it.

Then you brought Annette and I together again. Her young minister husband had died a month before Garth and she was left with three little children. We had much in common and that day we explored how our reluctance to be in the desert place bred restless discontent and the growing poison of resentment. I recall telling her that I challenged you in a way similar to the man on the cross beside you. 'If you are the son of God, save me.' Drinking the bitter cup may have been your idea of the way to life, Lord, but it certainly wasn't mine. I kept telling you that you had made a big mistake and you didn't know what was good for me or my children. I could clearly see how much my children needed love and how empty of it I was. I could see no good purpose being served by the mess we were in. I certainly couldn't see how your love and goodness was ever to be reflected in it. To accept the situation seemed utter folly. To believe that you might somehow be in the desert place working a good plan seemed a pipedream.

Yet you had led both Annette and I to Isaiah 43:19:

I will make a road through the wilderness
and give you streams of water there.

Your promise was given *in* the wilderness. The path and sustenance were found *in* that unlikely place.

Another verse you kept setting before me was Hosea 2:15: 'I will make Trouble Valley a door of hope.' I desperately wanted the door of hope, but you had real difficulty convincing me that it was to be found in Trouble Valley.

My head knowledge of Daniel and Joseph and of your own resurrection after the crucifixion didn't help. In the midst of it your acceptance of the cross was, to your friends, nothing short of folly. And I was in the midst – not a good place for clear vision. Even you, in the midst, asked your Father why he had left you. Yet what struck me with real force was that you did freely surrender to your Father and, even when feeling abandoned, you went right on to surrender your spirit to him. That's trust and that moved me.

Lord, I began to see how my lack of faith, my lack of trust, my lack of willingness to let go the resentment tightly clenched in my clammy hands, stopped you releasing the spring of water into my desert. I knew I was behaving as the Israelites did in captivity in Babylon. I had hung my harp on a willow tree and wept, 'How can I sing to you in a foreign land?' (see Psalm 137:4).

My conversations with John, Margaret, Annette and your Scripture, which tugged at my spirit with its own ring of truth, brought me face to face with a choice: to try to fight my way out of the desert back to the promised land as best I could believing this was a bad place – enemy territory, empty of you. Or to surrender to you in this new landscape, trusting you to be in it. That, I knew, meant letting those noisy destructive residents go and embracing acceptance as willingly as you embraced the cross.

I remember well the day I came to you holding in my tightly clenched fists the ashes of human enterprise. I knelt before you in my lounge. The drama of Easter unfolded in my mind. You hung on your cross, the light playing across your face and you looked at me. A flight of steps rose from me to you. You spoke those words so familiar to me, 'Come on up.' As I mounted each step I found them labelled with the very things your hands were spread to receive: anger, fear, resentment, jealousy, guilt, self-pity. I paused on each step and surrendered to you the twisted pieces of my life. I came longing to commit myself to your outstretched arms, yet fearful lest you fail me and further disillusionment destroy me. Each step forward lessened the fear until at the foot of the cross I gazed in love upon you, who loved me enough to spread your arms and die for me.

Lord, Easter that year took on a special meaning. New shafts of light penetrated the dark places in my spirit. I knew the key had turned; the door stood a fraction ajar. But Lord, we both knew wholeness was not yet complete. Prayer had given the eviction notice to my unsavoury guests. The process was underway, but it was a process. Those attitudes had been sending down roots for two years. They had become comfortable, though undesirable, lodgers and, in the following months when something touched a raw wound, it was all too easy to welcome back a twinge of anger, a seed of resentment, a jealous thought. Then the light dimmed. I had to surrender time and again to you.

That Easter prayer had been a real turning point and over the next four months, although I still felt as in a desert place, I was much more positive that you were there with me. Those months, Lord, were walked more by faith than any before or since. At last I actually trusted you, though I still could not see you clearly nor feel fully free. Lord, I really believe you honoured that trust by completing the process in a very special way, putting your love and power beyond all doubt.

Saturday, 23 August 1986 is a red-letter day on my calendar, Lord. Is that how you see it too? I believe it's as special to you as it is to me.

I woke early to the sound of rain on the roof. The children still slept. I made myself some tea and toast and took them back to bed. It was still dark and cold outside. I had woken to a sickening reality striking my stomach like a stone sinking to the muddy floor of a stagnant pond.

Give Me Your Cloak

I asked you again for the umpteenth time, 'God, where am I headed? Where are you? I've caught fleeting glimpses of you since Easter, but elusive as mercury. I stumble through each day blind and longing to see you again.' I remembered someone else who had been blind, not in spirit, but blind nonetheless. I found Bartimaeus in Mark's Gospel.

Laying aside my breakfast tray and propping myself in a comfortable position to concentrate, I took up the story of this man sitting in darkness and I read it aloud slowly, setting the scene firmly in my mind, shutting my eyes and praying to you in deep earnest, 'Lord, please meet me.' I put myself in Bartimaeus' place. Did you know what would happen, Lord? I didn't. It was very dark. I could feel the rough road but see nothing. I sat enveloped in my heavy cloak, confused by the movement and noise on the road. I heard your name mentioned, 'Jesus.' I couldn't identify you. I just knew you were leaving town and intense fear gripped me that if I couldn't get to you now I would remain forever blind and spiritually bankrupt, begging on a deserted road.

In despair I called your name, 'Jesus.' I called again above the noise of the crowd, 'Jesus.' You stopped and called to me, 'Elsa.' I've never heard my name spoken with such love. I tossed my cloak aside and hurried towards your voice. I felt your hands take mine and I heard your penetrating question, 'What do you want me to do for you?'

My heart pounded. I blurted out, 'Can you really do something? I want to see you, Lord. Just to be able to see you. I can't follow when I can't see.'

Suddenly I saw your hands that held mine and looked into your loving eyes that searched my face. Your next words surprised me.

'Bring me your cloak.'

It lay on the roadside where I had thrown it in my haste to get to you.

'You want it, Lord?' I asked. Hesitantly I brought it to you. Now I could see how heavy, ugly and black it was. Then I saw it had pockets and they were labelled. There was one labelled jealousy, with pictures of happy couples, fulfilled Christians and people living purposeful lives. There was a pocket bulging with resentment at Garth's death, my new home, the pain of conflict, financial burdens and solo decision making. There was a small pocket labelled guilt that I carried for being inadequate, unfaithful to you Lord, and blind. There was a large pocket of self-pity that I wished I could hide from you but I guess you knew all about that too, and the whole cloak was labelled around the hem with the word depression. I was so ashamed of it and so reluctant to give it to you Jesus. You just waited. Finally, I passed it to you. You put it on.

I watched in horror as you turned and walked to your cross weighed down by my cloak. I wanted to stop you. I wanted to cry out, 'Don't, Lord. It's all mine and you don't deserve that pain.' But I was speechless. As you hung there an amazing thing happened. My cloak dissolved into your very flesh and blood, every ugly pocket becoming you and, as you died, I broke inside and wept in deep repentance for what I had done to you. Then a huge sense of relief flooded me. My cloak was gone and absolutely irretrievable. I stood on the road and wept tears of mingled repentance and relief.

When I finally raised my tear-stained face you stood before me alive and well, a knowing smile on your face, and you draped about my shoulders a soft, light cloak for the journey we would share together. Somehow I was not surprised to find that the pockets in this new cloak labelled patience, joy, love, self-control, kindness, peace were empty. I'd been empty of those for a long time. Just one pocket over my heart, labelled hope, contained a tiny seed just germinating and I felt the warmth of its growing enter my body. I stood before you straight, unencumbered, ready to follow. I knew it meant moving on, leaving my familiar begging position at the roadside. I held no regrets for I could see you and I was free at last. What joy!

You, Lord, probably know better than I how long it took me to become aware of the blankets around me, the pillow I leaned against, the several wet hankies I'd saturated as I'd truly wept in repentance. And the joy still bubbled within.

It bubbled for days to follow. You had truly met me and given me back my sight. I really could not believe the transformation. I kept expecting the bubble to burst. Yet each morning I woke with the joy still there and after a week I stopped doubting you, Lord, and began to thank you for the wonder of it all; for your accepting my poisonous negative attitudes and setting me free.

I used to wonder why you would be bothered with anyone's ugly cloak and the pain it meant for you, but if you experienced only half the joy that I experienced in my new freedom I can see why you bother. I believe it gave you real delight to see my energy return. I really discovered a truth Peter knew all about but somehow I'd missed completely.

> Repent, then, and turn to God, so that he will forgive your sins. If you do, times of spiritual strength will come from the Lord...
> (Acts 3:19, 20)

Lord, you watched my weariness, discouragement and my striving to restore flagging zeal. You knew my sin was a key reason and you helped me surrender it. Hundreds of years ago David understood well the debilitating effect of unconfessed sin.

> When I did not confess my sins, I was worn out
> my strength was completely drained
> (Psalm 32:3, 4)

Lord, in that precious time you gave me a new understanding of confession, not as a ghastly duty to perform like regular doses of castor oil, but as the gateway to wholeness, the key to freedom, the only way to dispel the dark and to see you again.

I have to admire your wonderful sense of timing, Lord. You knew my new level of energy was about to be well tested just two weeks later.

August school holidays arrived. The children were registered for an Inter School Christian Fellowship bike tour, their third in as many years, seven days and 260 kilometres of tough, hilly back country roads. This time I intended to join them – not, I might add, on a bicycle, but as assistant cook to Leonie. Lord, you knew my anxiety at the prospect of cooking for forty hungry teenagers, shifting kitchens each day and setting up roadside lunch stops. You were well aware of the reserves of energy

I would require. My shoulders ached from lifting heavy boxes of food, large pots and trestles. My evening prayers to you hung unfinished as sleep overtook me, leaving me quite oblivious to you, the ridges in the floor of the van and the breathing of Aneta and Katrina snuggled in sleeping bags beside me in the confined space.

The long hard days brought physical weariness but spiritual exhilaration. I shared your joy in watching those young people study and pray together, worship and play. They were extended physically and spiritually and I saw you grow in them and them in you.

After emotional goodbyes between kids and the claiming of assorted tea towels, parkas and muddy bikes, I drove home with my children and a week's dirty washing, muddy enough to tax any modern washing powder. I thought of the dirty cloak you had taken from me and completely transformed.

> Remove my sin, and I will be clean;
> wash me, and I will be whiter than snow.
> (Psalm 51:7)

You beat washing powder any day, Lord. As I pulled up the drive a new wave of joy burst upon me. This was home and I was glad to see it. It looked comfortable and inviting. All resentment had gone and for the first time in two years genuine gratitude took its place. Acceptance had arrived as a daisy. Deep praise to you was born. You had indeed set me free, enabling me to take my 'harp down from the willow tree' and sing to you:

> Just like you promised, you've come.
> Just like you told me, you're here.
> And my desire is that you know
> I love you, I worship you,
> I welcome you here.[6]

Garth and Elsa after
Garth's ordination, 1969.

The church in Naseby where
Garth and Elsa were married in 1967.

A drawing by Garth
of the manse in Feilding, 1982.

Elsa, Garth, Ian, Jim,
Katrina and Aneta, 1982.

St Paul's, Feilding,
the day of Garth's funeral, 1985.

Elsa and her children
at their new home in Feilding, 1986.

Elsa with her new book, 2001.

Elsa and her children at the
wedding of Katrina and Tim, 2001.

Aneta, Bevan and Tayla, 1996.

Elsa with her grandchildren
Tayla and Avon, 2002.

Garth, 1982.

chapter
fourteen

WITH LOVE FROM GOD

Our God has an enormous capacity for love and the most creative ways of expressing it. When Garth and I first met we expressed our love in age-old patterns. In marriage, and especially after a marriage enrichment weekend, we sought creative ways to say 'I love you'.

Garth's work took him away from home occasionally. Often, on such occasions, I would slip into the empty bed and discover a precious message tucked under my pillow.

Once, when Garth was away for ten days, I promised to send him a wagonload of love and prayers with each goods train that sped by our home. He assured me that 200 kilometres north, each time he heard the train he felt warmed and encouraged by my love. Those who drove the trains had no idea of the precious links they made for us each day.

Garth knew my love for flowers. Once he presented me with a stem of miniature orchids from the fernery, ten times smaller than florists' ones; many times more precious. On another occasion, after the girls and I returned from a holiday, Garth and the boys gave us a royal welcome and there on the TV was the most original flower arrangement I have ever seen. It followed none of the rules for balance, colour or harmony, but it spelled 'L O V E' in capital letters.

We sent special telegrams to each other with messages hidden from the postal service. We planned creative birthday parties, once using the whole house for a progressive dinner. In countless ways we tried to be creative in our love; to say, 'You're special. I care.' But we could never outdo God for creativity. He is both the master of creativity and the author of love. I discovered this powerfully in the two years following Garth's death.

When Garth died I caught a glimpse of God's tender love in preparing me for this event. I encountered his powerful love in the healing of our memories. His comforting love was reflected in the hundreds of warm letters that winged their way to our home in the days that followed Garth's death. Busy days terminated in dreadful silence and the emptiness of our double bed echoed the emptiness inside me. I rolled over to fill the space Garth had previously occupied. To break the lonely silence I read the many letters that had arrived and been put aside in the busyness of the day. Curled up in bed, I savoured each beautiful letter and felt so close to our friends. I was kept company for many nights. Their words filled the silence.

Later, when the volume of mail diminished, I met each of those friends again at bedtime as I wrote replies. The companionship and writing were warm and healing. God comforted me.

I am privileged to have friends who didn't just send sympathy cards, but who took time to reflect on Garth's life, to recall precious and, sometimes, hilarious events. Such letters were a real ministry to me and to the children who discovered new things about their dad. Those letters gave them a treasure chest of memories to dip into any time.

In spite of all the letters I felt strangely vulnerable, afraid that friendships formed through the common task of ministry would not survive. God knew my fear. He had the answer. Some of those dear friends continued to correspond regularly. When nothing else in my life seemed ongoing, those letters were precious. They assured me of continued friendship and love.

In this regard my sister, Valerie, was incredible. I met God time and again in her letters. Late each Sunday evening she wrote letters to me which, when they appeared in my box on Wednesday, not only told me that Valerie cared, but also said from God, 'I love you. I understand.' When we moved house she wrote three times in one week, and included with her letters a treasured bookmark, a promise God had given her for me and a verse of Scripture. Thus she provided stability and made my transplanting so much easier to bear.

Recently a friend expressed regret that he lived too far away to keep personal contact with his newly widowed Mum. I asked if he could write. Like many men he didn't enjoy writing. I suggested he do it anyway. 'Write about the kids, work, the weather, write "I love you. I care," anything, but write regularly for at least six months – the time when the silence echoes the loneliness of her life. Let her find in her letterbox words to fill the silence of her days, to soften the harsh reality, to touch her life in a life where touch has vanished.'

I knew the hunger for touch. How I missed Garth's loving embrace. In ministry we had recognised the healing power of touch and witnessed that people deprived of touch were starved of something essential to wholeness. I remember from years past a story of a little girl and her Mum who were walking down a dark, tree-lined path when Mum realised she had left behind something she needed. She asked the little girl to wait while she ran back. The child was nervous, 'But I'll be all alone,' she pleaded.

Her mum tried to reassure her, 'Jesus will be with you. He promises never to leave you.'

The little girl was quick with her reply, 'But I'd rather have someone with skin on.' I, too, needed someone with skin on. That is exactly what Jesus has provided in the 'body of Christ'. God first met human need in the incarnation – 'God in flesh'. Then Jesus sent his disciples with the words, 'As the Father sent me, so I send you' (John 20:21). He has sent his body, his people, to be God in flesh. If Christ dwells in his people, by his Spirit, then his people are Christ with skin on in this needy world.

The people of God, male and female, who hugged me and held me when I cried, brought Jesus' love to me and helped to ease a deep physical hunger within me.

I believe many lonely people in the world try to satisfy that hunger with sex because they have no place where they can receive physical touch

Shattered and Restored

that is akin to the love of God, freely given, unconditional, pure and healing.

I experienced God's arms around me in his beautiful people and I knew their love and his. That doesn't rule out the possibility that Jesus himself may touch me in a way that is almost physical. He has. At times his presence has been so real I have experienced his warm embrace in a physical way.

In my most painful times I needed people's warm presence much more than I needed their advice. Initially, I was not ready for sweeping solutions. In fact, subconsciously, I avoided becoming self-sufficient for fear I would be left alone.

Garth had discovered, in ministry, that some people resist all suggested solutions to their problems because the problems are only symptoms. The underlying ache is for companionship, love and acceptance. Solving problems may only lead to further isolation.

I found that contact was more helpful, initially, than counsel. Jesus, in his distress in the garden, did not seek counsel but companionship. 'Could you not watch with me one hour?' (Matthew 26:40 RSV). He didn't ask that they come up with a solution, just that they keep him company.

I am eternally grateful to those who watched with me, helpless as they felt, and kept me company. They had few words to offer. Words seemed empty anyway; even, to my dismay, the Word of God. Statements like, 'God works all things together for good,' felt hollow. The Christians who approached my pain with a 'Praise the Lord, anyway' effervescence left me feeling both guilty and angry. I rejected Scripture quoted at me. Yet I discovered that God and some of his people knew how to feed me the true, living Word in palatable ways. They gave it gift-wrapped in love. They had discovered the wisdom of the words, 'I don't care how much you know, until I know how much you care.'

The Lord gently fed me his Word of life and healing. He didn't once ram it down my throat. He let the words settle quietly in my spirit, or drift across my mind, that I might savour them – no compulsion, pure invitation.

When a person is physically sick one offers them, not a plateful of high fibre, but a little ice cream, or a savoury morsel easily digested. The Lord gave me dainty morsels from his Word, that satisfied my deep hunger. I was hungry for love and he satisfied me.

These passages I savoured often:

'For one brief moment I left you;
with deep love I will take you back
 ...I will show you my love forever.'
So says the LORD who saves you.
'The mountains and hills may crumble,
but my love for you will never end;
I will keep forever my promise of peace.'
So says the Lord who loves you.
(Isaiah 54:7, 8, 10)

Even if a mother forgets her child,
I will never forget you.
...I can never forget you!
I have written your name on the palms of my hands.
(Isaiah 49:15, 16)

How can I give you up...?
How can I abandon you?
...My heart will not let me do it!
My love for you is too strong.
(Hosea 11:8)

The Lord says, 'I will bring my people back to me.
I will love them with all my heart.
Once again they will live under my protection.
They will be fruitful like a vineyard.
Like an evergreen tree I will shelter them;
I am the source of all their blessings.'
(Hosea 14:4, 7, 8)

The people of God can choose from the well-stocked pantry of his Word a diet that meets the needs of hurting people. That is not being selective. It is being sensitive, loving and Christlike. When people are down, words that encourage are called for before the hard words of challenge and service.

I believe the Word of God is to be used, not as a sledge-hammer to knock a person back into line, but as a love song to woo a person back to the one who loves them most. God said, 'I am going to take her into the desert again; there I will win her back with words of love' (Hosea 2:14). God's way with wounded people is with gentle, persuasive, persistent love. Listen to Jesus' job description from Isaiah 42.

> He will not shout or raise his voice
> or make loud speeches in the streets.
> He will not break off a bent reed
> nor put out a flickering lamp.
> He will not lose hope or courage...
> (Isaiah 42:2, 3, 4)

It's difficult, in the darkness, to hang on to hope. It's important to know that Jesus hasn't lost hope and this is confirmed when God's people reflect the same hope. Most helpful to me were people who believed in me when I no longer did. I used to visit Shiloh, a Christian community, because there, in my friends Marjory and Ron, I saw a deep hope in God and an unfailing belief that, with Christ, I would 'make it'. They embodied those servant words from Isaiah 42.

It takes a lot of hope and courage to 'hang in there' for a long time with one suffering deep loss. My friends fielded my anger, yet never grew resentful, nor gave up. They didn't withdraw when they felt inadequate. They listened to my confusion till they must have been heartily sick of it. They stayed by me and gave me the precious gift of their hope and their courage.

I know a beautiful Christian lady whose young husband died very suddenly. In the natural anger that is a part of grief, she lashed out at all who tried to help. One by one her church family gave up on her until, in bitter anger, she turned her back on Jesus and all she had believed. If only they had fulfilled the job description of the servant of God, their courage would have absorbed her anger without retaliation and their hope and faith may have eventually won her back through love. She didn't see Jesus in them when she most needed to.

What is not always understood by people who offer love to one in pain, is that the loving actions may be received with mixed reactions of pain and joy. Warm appreciation is not always the first response; sometimes it is quite the reverse. The love will be rejected and, if the giver does not understand why, resentment may result.

Let me illustrate. Deeply caring families invited us to share meals with them. I recognised their love, yet initially, I found those occasions incredibly painful. The presence of husbands and wives sharing meal preparation and conversation threw my loss into stark relief and I wanted to run away.

People regularly asked how I was. The question was asked out of love and concern, but I was sick of updating people. It only highlighted my loneliness.

Others said, 'If you need any help, let me know.' Diminished confidence wouldn't allow me to ask. To confess need was just one more death blow to my self-worth. They may well be forgiven for supposing I rejected their love. No. I saw their love. I just couldn't take up the offer without adding to the pain.

One day a young widowed friend rose in the morning to find several strong men turning over her vegetable garden. Her response was not one of gratitude, but of intense anger. Unwittingly they had trodden all over her pride, her need for privacy and her already damaged ego. How were they to know? They were only trying to care. Even a warm hug, something I hungered for, sometimes heightened awareness of all I had lost.

I learned that to remain open to love meant being vulnerable to pain as well. A cursory glance at Jesus' life should have shown me that. I learned to stay open to people's expressions of love, to be deeply grateful and, when wounded, to give it to Jesus.

A friend called one day with a specific offer of help. I was really touched by the thoughtfulness and accepted gratefully. He commented jovially, 'Oh, that's okay. We have to look after you widow ladies.' That comment cut to the core and I was tempted to throw his offer in his face. Comments that once would have washed over me now stung. Just as a cut finger responds violently to being bumped so, too, my wounded emotions reacted strongly to thoughtless comments. Yet, I knew he cared. To reject his offer would have been to shut out love.

If you are in that place of needing love, yet feeling vulnerable, I make a strong plea to you to stay open, be grateful, go on receiving, even when it's humiliating, difficult and makes you vulnerable. Receive love in all its expressions and you will stay open to the author of all love, God himself. If some expression of love is totally inappropriate for you, you may need to gently say so, while still expressing appreciation for the thoughtfulness. Maybe you can say what is helpful for you? How can anyone be expected to guess? We are all so different.

If you are one desiring to offer love in action, please tread gently. Be specific in your offers, but allow the right to decline – respect the individual. As Jesus offers himself to us but often awaits our permission to enter, do the same for your friend. Your love may be thrown back in your face. Forgive and recognise that such action is the measure of pain and a clear indication that your love is greatly needed; not your pity, nor your condemnation, but your warm, unshakeable acceptance and patient hope and courage.

I was greatly encouraged by the very practical offers of help I received. The nebulous, 'If you want anything, ask me,' was not particularly helpful. On the other hand, the minister who called and said, 'When you move, would you like me to come and attend to any wiring, light fittings, etc. you may need? I'd just love to exercise my electrician's skills again,' made it very easy to accept. Likewise, the friends who dug up and replaced all the drains, teaching my boys new skills in the process and making them feel part of a team effort, were a real blessing. The local Salvation Army Officer changed uniform for overalls one day and repaired bicycles.

All those gifts of time and skill heightened the pain I experienced at my inadequacy, but they brought great joy as well. And behind each gift was my loving heavenly Father saying, 'I love you. Receive my love, delivered through my people.'

A widow of five years, aware that widowhood brings loss of social life, invited me out to a restaurant meal. What a special gift that was. Another thoughtful friend, appreciating that loneliness engulfed me when the children left for school each day, called frequently just after they left, dried dishes or hung washing with me and then continued on her way, having delivered her love letter from God.

Single adults offered me a special gift. They could give me companionship when married couples were busy with their families. It was not that I needed counsel. I simply needed a friend, one who would sit and have coffee, play scrabble, or watch a TV programme. When the boys were busy with homework or out, and the girls were asleep, my friends, Jane and Lorraine, filled empty evenings with their comfortable companionship.

My very special prayer partner, Leonie, offered deep companionship and something more. We not only talked and prayed together, but we also sometimes worked together. Garth's death had brought a sudden end to shared tasks. I found it lonely tackling tasks by myself. Leonie joined me in gardening, bottling fruit and the daunting task of re-upholstering my sofa. We had a lot of fun, working side by side.

God is creative and generous in his loving. His people were also. The anonymous gift that enabled the boys to attend Easter camp, the cheque for plants for my garden, the gifts to finance our South Island holiday, all spoke of a generous people who reflected our generous God.

I was amazed at the people who remembered my birthday. I wanted to forget it. What was there to celebrate if I couldn't share it with Garth? Yet their love won through. Little gifts, sprays of flowers, a carefully chosen card, a visit, a special phone call from Garth's parents, all absorbed the pain and changed a potentially dreadful day into a priceless gift.

God's love reached me through his people. I believe it is the main way in which God reaches deeply hurting people, especially those who are angry at God in their grief. The love of his people, genuine, persistent and gentle, eventually melted my anger and opened a way back to receive the love of God. But God also touched me directly with his love. He touched my children too. For instance, four weeks after Garth's death, Aneta was drying dishes with me and she casually said, 'I saw Daddy last night. God woke me up and he was there.'

'Tell me about it,' I said, intrigued.

She went on, 'I was asleep and God woke me up. I just knew it was him. Daddy was standing at the bottom of my bed. He had on his church clothes and his glasses and his real hair. I thought he was a ghost for a moment, but he was real.'

'Were you afraid?'

'Oh, no.'

'Did he say anything?'

'No, he just smiled at me. Then after a while he went away. He just wasn't there.'

'How did you feel?' I asked.

'Good,' she replied. 'Really good.'

I told her that God must love her very much to allow her to see her Daddy and now she could always carry that lovely memory of his warm smile, know that he was well, and that he loved her.

I reflected on her description of Garth. She had been adamant that he had his real hair and glasses on. Why mention those? Then I remembered that the only time she had ever seen him without glasses was in death and then he had no wig either. Her last memory of her Daddy had been very bad. God knew that and touched her with this special loving gift. Her Daddy, smiling at her from the end of her bed, was well and strong, looking as she had experienced him in life and not as she had seen him in death. I love my Lord who pays so much attention to the needs of a little girl in her grief.

He paid attention to my grief too, handling it in ways appropriate for me. In the months following Garth's death, I withdrew to nurse my wounded spirit. Yet frequently, God would bring to my attention someone with a deep need and issue me with the invitation to shift my focus to the other, to be his instrument in bringing his love and healing. And every time I did, I also opened the door for God to reach to me, for I could not clench my fists and imprison my spirit and still be a channel of God's grace to someone else. The moment I sought God's love, grace and power for another, he not only met them powerfully, but bathed my wounds as well. A great deal of healing took place in me, not as I sought ministry, but as I lost myself in meeting another with Jesus' love. Some people assumed I had enough pain of my own without needing to take other people's problems on board. But, in fact, ministry never added to my burden. It always reduced it. Loving others, opening myself to be a channel for God's grace, was always freeing and brought great joy. I saw God act in people's lives and heard again his promise to be active in mine.

The first anniversary of Garth's death was a day of receiving the love of God's people and also a chance to do something for another. My nephew, Colin, was with us. Garth's death had shattered his twenty-first birthday celebrations the previous year. Now, on his twenty-second birthday, I prepared a special party for him. It gave me great joy, as did the visits of friends, phone calls and gifts of flowers. All day long God's love surrounded me. I enjoyed the fun of the party, the fresh sparkle in Aneta's eyes and the children's delight. Late that evening I wrote to God of the joy in my heart:

One whole year, Lord.
In some ways it seems a million.
All day long you assembled a bouquet for me,
Each bloom arranged with care;
Phone calls, letters, visits and cards;
Beautiful flowers and warm words;
A party to celebrate.
And when it was all arranged
I recognised your creative hand in it;
Your words on the card – *I care for you.*
I love you dearly.
Receive my love.
...your Father God

chapter
fifteen

THE MORNING CHORUS

The verandah rail is broad and comfortable. I love to sit on it and lean against the sturdy roughcast wall. Before me the home paddock, sloping away to the road, is planted with a variety of majestic English trees.

Atop the twisted weeping elm a thrush trills forth its morning song. From the ancient macrocarpa a blackbird calls out his territory. Magpies chortle from the pines on the next ridge, their voices carried on the morning air and, woven through this orchestra, come the sweet strains of the grey warbler and the gentle twitter of a fantail.

I love this old homestead, Glen Innes, in its magnificent gardens. Last night, as darkness fell, the birds gave their evening concerto and I was drawn to the verandah to listen. I came here to write. Away from exuberant teenagers, telephone and household tasks. I chose this place because it's quiet and I could be alone. Yet I feared the loneliness as I drove up yesterday. The children, Garth and I had always holidayed here together. As I sat on the verandah rail last evening at twilight I could see Garth in his corduroy pants sitting on the bank, with ten-year-old Ian playing the cornet. I saw little Aneta in pink togs and blond pigtails eager to be taken swimming and Garth helping Katrina to line up a snooker ball when she was still only a fraction taller than the table. Then I saw Garth resting in a deck chair, cup of tea beside him on the verandah rail, the children on the steps chomping crunchy apples, the sun streaming in on us, refreshing our exhausted spirits and bodies. I missed him and I wept for I wanted to grow old together with him and now I sat alone on the verandah rail.

But the tears were brief, the pain sharp but short. As the night embraced the homestead and stilled the birds, my Lord wrapped me in his love and stilled the ache. I was not alone and his peace infused me.

Reluctantly, I had left my verandah perch as the night air cooled, to curl up by the glowing fire and listen to the crackle of burning macrocarpa logs and feel the warmth embrace me. My toes had wriggled in the sheepskin rug and my fingers burrowed into its softness. The peace in my spirit deepened.

Alone in this huge old house, yet not alone. I felt the Lord in the quiet evening, in the sound of thirsty ground soaking up welcome rain, in the life of the glowing fire, the warmth of the soft rug and, as I snuggled into bed late last night, my heart was glad that my Lord was in this place and would lead me in the days ahead to pen a love letter that will encourage others to enter a new intimacy with him.

This morning the hills are shrouded in mist, symbolic of the veil I feel still covers the last chapter of my book. I'll wait for the Lord to roll away his clouds and show me the detail of this chapter. Meanwhile, the foreground is in sharp relief; the trees framed against the white mist. Jesus, too, seems to stand in sharp relief this morning as if he wants me to focus only on him for this moment, my heart linked with his in praise. In short, to lean on my comfortable verandah rail and join this morning chorus.

This quiet gladness and intimacy with Jesus was not a part of my life four years ago. It's God's answer to the burning question of singleness. Actually, I believe it's God's answer for every human being, for we are designed for intimacy with God, but as long as we can be reasonably fulfilled in human relationships we, sadly, relegate him to a back seat. It has been my joy to discover that intimacy with God is the key to maintaining and experiencing the real joy of all other relationships.

For seventeen years Garth had met most of my needs for intimacy.

With his death, I was more lonely than I care to remember. I've already shared something of the hunger for physical intimacy that followed bereavement.

In marriage the two become one flesh. With the death of one the other feels torn in half and aching to be completed. I questioned whether God could bring wholeness in this area. After all he said, 'It is not good for man to be alone' (Genesis 2:18). Would I always have to live with this deep ache? My logic presented four options.

1. I could deny my sexuality and bury my feelings. I was sure that would lead to emotional trouble and, anyway, I actually couldn't do it.
2. I could seek out a new partner. But, for now, I didn't want to. It was Garth I hungered for and I wanted his rich companionship that expressed itself in many more ways than sexual intimacy.
3. I could seek sexual union outside of a marriage commitment. That was both abhorrent to me and to God. Sex is only one facet of the intimacy found in a loving relationship and is utterly impoverished outside of a genuine commitment to one another in marriage.
4. God could have the answer. Didn't his Word say, 'And with all his abundant wealth through Christ Jesus, my God will supply all your needs' (Philippians 4:19).

He didn't supply an answer immediately. I probably wouldn't have been able to hear it then anyway. But, like other words from him, I hung onto that verse when it didn't seem to be true any more and kept asking him how he could make it real for me.

Physical loss and desire usually arrived as stealthily, yet forcefully, as a tidal wave breaking upon a sleeping village. An elderly couple passed me in the park one day hand in hand and that simple action tugged at my heart and opened a still raw wound. A couple left their children with me and went to celebrate a wedding anniversary. Their joy in each other pierced my heart. The film *Children of a Lesser God,* highlighted a passionate relationship and left me longing for Garth's physical presence and hammering at the gates of heaven with my often-voiced question, 'God, can you heal this wound? Can you comfort me?'

And he did. One experience I will always remember. This particular evening I curled up in bed and, as usual, drew the day to a close by saying goodnight to God, acknowledging his protection and love. Mentally, I focused on his presence. Suddenly, I sensed God at the side of my bed. I felt a gentle warm hand on my shoulder. I knew he smiled at me. Then, what I can only describe as 'his loving presence', embraced me. Words cannot describe the peace that filled me. I knew God was there, not because Scripture or my head said so, but because I had felt and experienced his love in physical form. He gave me the priceless gift of a heart awareness that cannot be shaken.

Over the months, as God restored my relationship with himself, he gave me glimpses of his incredible love for me and extended an invitation to come into a greater intimacy with himself. At the same time he began to help me see the different types of intimacy we experience as human beings and to help me to develop those in healthy healing ways. Sex is only one expression of intimacy.

With Garth's death I was bereft of other intimacies as well. I hungered for stimulating intellectual intimacy – sharing a world of ideas. I missed recreational intimacy; times of playing together, whether scrabble or model trains. The creative intimacy of shared gardening was gone. I missed the aesthetic intimacy of a common taste in music – my children don't share my musical tastes. And poignantly absent was emotional intimacy; being in tune with another and knowing he was in tune with me. Work intimacy was obviously missing. We had shared ministry and homemaking for seventeen years.

Graciously, God brought across my path different people with whom I could develop some of those intimacies. With Lorraine, I enjoy scrabble, sharing a movie and listening to music. I have a rich spiritual intimacy with my prayer partner, Leonie, and others in my church family. I have friends with whom I share ordinary tasks.

I believe we are only whole as we develop as many intimacies as possible. One person cannot meet them all, even in marriage, but for the single person, it's really important to have a range of relationships which will meet the different kinds of intimacy hungered for.

Having said all that, I have discovered time and again that, as I have reached out to another, my own need has been met. If I just make a list of my needs for intimacy and set out to get them met I will be disappointed every time because, when the focus is self, something dies inside. When my focus goes out, there's an open door for blessing to flow back in.

The same applies to my intimacy with God. When I called to him out of my deep need he was there for me, but I really couldn't receive all he longed to give. As I've grown to the place where I love him just for himself something flows over back to me and my deep joy is the result not of seeking for it, but of being lost in my love for him.

So have I completely resolved the question of singleness and sexuality? No. That was brought home forcefully a little over a year ago.

The music was playing softly as I settled myself in the quiet church for the pre-Easter service. The afternoon had been rushed as children packed and left for Easter camp. Excited greetings and warm hugs exchanged, luggage stuffed into bulging baggage racks and they were off. Now I could be still and meet my Lord.

I closed my eyes to focus on the words and music drawing us into meditation. But suddenly, another scene filled my mind. Garth walked across the church platform, old brown briefcase in hand and stepped up to the lectern to lead worship. The reality was so powerful I opened my eyes. Mark, our minister, sat quietly at the front, absorbed in meditation. The scene still played in my mind. All my senses awakened, memories flooded back – the scent of Garth, his characteristic movements, the way he grasped the lectern, and snippets of his favourite songs of worship rang in my ears. I shook my head and tried to direct my attention back to the music drifting out of the speakers, but nothing would stop the replay of years of worship led by Garth in this church and anguish welled within me. He was so real, so present, so familiar and yet so out of reach.

I was still struggling with physical hunger for Garth when the service ended. People chatted in small groups about the church. I looked for someone who would hold me while I cried. They were all occupied.

Shattered and Restored

I fled into the night, slid into my van and wrapping my arms around the cold steering wheel, let the tears flow in release to God.

I had worshipped in that church for three years without being caught in such intensity of desire. In the beginning I had cried to God, 'What do I do with it? Do you have any answers?' Three years had taught me some of his answers. He had led me to develop warm healthy intimacies with many people and with himself. He had taught me to release pain. I could still be knocked off balance. Only I recovered more rapidly with the Lord's help. I couldn't prevent the ache of incompleteness, but I was further along the track in knowing how to handle it.

I avoid sensuous books and movies, and situations that highlight all I miss, or stimulate desire. I can't deny my sexuality. That would be to deny what God created. I have learned to accept it as a gift and to acknowledge the pain of unfulfilment, and share that reality with God. I believe God wants me to harness sexual energy into positive creative activity; especially into being present for others in loving ways. For physical union is simply one expression of the fullness of love and, for the single person, love must find other creative expression. I continue to grow in intimacy with my Lord. As I love God more completely and am able to live more fully in his love, I come into wholeness in every aspect of my being. As I experience the exuberant love of God cascading over me my whole body rejoices.

I know that what affects my body affects my spirit and the converse is, therefore, also true. When my spirit was crushed, my body ached. When my body hungered for fulfilment, my spirit languished wounded. But when I come into an intimacy of love with my Lord and experience the fullness of his love, my spirit soars and my body pulsates with health and energy. Then I am complete in a way that only God can make possible.

God may not explain my ache or take it all away, but he does fill it with his presence. And that presence is infinitely richer than anything I experienced four years ago. Through grief I have grown into a deeper intimacy with God than I knew was possible. Early in the process the new growth was not recognised by some, nor always by me either. Two years ago a professional friend spoke of my relationship with God as being dead because anger appeared to have replaced love. He did me a great favour with his challenge. 'People with dead relationships don't argue,' I contended. 'They don't get angry. They don't talk. My relationship with God is very much alive and very vocal. I'm yelling at him.' My friend raised his eyebrows. How could I love God and be angry with him? 'Simple. It's wounded love that breeds such anger.' In C. S. Lewis' words, 'Such anger is the fluid that love bleeds when you cut it.' That's true in precious marriages and loving families and it was true of me with God. That day I clearly saw my love for God behind the anger and I believed our relationship would weather the storm.

My son, Jim, and I had some turbulent times last year. After one heated argument he came to me to apologise, 'Mum,' he said, 'when I can't handle my frustration with myself any more I spill it all over you because, with you, I am safe.' Yes, I got hurt at his anger, but what a compliment about the quality of our relationship.

Likewise with God, I knew I was safe and he would not reject me. I took my anger to my heavenly parent who showed me on the cross that he was perfectly able to carry all my pain. He neither throws it back nor passes it on. He buries it. It's the end of the line. Then he resurrects something beautiful out of it into the bargain.

So I can proclaim with confidence now, 'My God does supply all my needs.' He has always supplied my needs, though I didn't always see the provision while I was blinded by the emotional storm and my preconceived ideas as to the form his provision should take.

When we moved house I longed for a secluded place away from family activity to meet with God and I mourned the loss of the church environment which had been so perfect. Yet eighteen months later, as I wandered into the garden shed for something, I paused; an inner voice prompting me to be still a moment. I settled on a bale of fresh straw and looked about me. God began to speak into my spirit, 'Do you see it now – your quiet place. Look about you. Let it speak to you of me. I will meet you in this ordinary, yet holy place. Listen to me.'

I looked about me with awe and wonder. It seemed as if two years of my life was assembled in that shed. The spades and forks told of the new ground the Lord and I had turned in my life, garden stakes spoke of the support I had been given when vulnerable, sprays and drain pipes told of the poisonous attitudes God had helped eliminate in me – the bitterness, resentment and choking fear he'd cleared and drained out. On the far shelf sat rows of shining bottles, some full of preserved fruit, and I knew he was restoring fruit in my life and filling the emptiness with good produce by his Spirit. Everything in that shed had a message of promise and, as I looked out across the lawn past the fruit trees and felt the warm sun slanting across the floor, I acknowledged to my Lord that I had missed his provision of a quiet place because it had come in a different form and I had not been ready for new things. Now this shed is a favourite place to take my Bible and be alone.

In quiet God satisfies me and equips me as parent. His is the energy and wisdom I draw on. In wonderful ways he has met each of my children.

Back in 1985 he promised to father them. I am constantly amazed at the creative ways he does that. Little gems stand out in my mind.

Running late one day, I left a note for eleven-year-old Aneta returning from school to have a sleep before a late night outing. Alone in the house she wrote to Jesus:

I am lying down all on my own.
There's no one here
no one there.
But then I hear a little voice in my heart.
It's saying to me, 'You're not alone, Jesus is in your heart.'
I woke up quickly.
I thought to myself, 'That is true.'
So read it now and you will see
That God is in my heart.
Wake up quick, think to yourself and you will see
That it is true.

One day I was sharing a book by David Watson with Jim. I chuckled as I added, 'I had a real twinge of jealousy as I thought of Garth and David sharing their similar theologies in heaven. I'd love to eavesdrop a while. I suppose that's a peculiar thought.'

He looked thoughtful, then replied carefully, 'I used to think of heaven as being out there somewhere. Now I believe it's closer than my hands and feet. Sometimes I almost feel Dad saying, "Well done, Jim"'

Where I initially feared for my children's faith I've seen them planted firmly in Jesus.

God has proved himself equal to every situation. He has not always done things the way I would (he probably knows better) and his provision has come in many creative ways. I have to learn not to dictate how he should provide or be blind to his answers by my preconceptions as I was in the case of my garden shed. I have to remember that God has the whole of creation at his disposal and all the creatures as well. He may, and often does, choose to use people to meet our needs, but he can also provide supernatural answers when they are appropriate. I've experienced both.

I look at how God met Jesus' human need for companionship in his twelve close friends whom he dearly loved. Yet when they all abandoned him before his death he could say, 'You will be scattered, each to his own home, and I will be left all alone. But I am not really alone, because the Father is with me' (John 16:32).

I'm not saying God is the final backup when human support fails. God was there in the beginning providing the human support and God was there when there was none left. God is the source and he will find a way if we will just not limit him by our small minds.

On the way to Glen Innes I stopped at a friend's place. Twenty minutes later I couldn't start the car. The verdict: a flat battery. Directed to an auto electrician, I waited while he tested and changed batteries. He was friendly and asked what I was doing in this part of the country. I'm never quite sure how people will react when I tell them I'm writing a book about my faith walk with God after the death of my husband.

'That's the question, isn't it? Where the hell is God?' was his strong response. He's had reason to ask it because of a recent family tragedy he told me of. He would identify with the writer of Psalm 77.

Will the Lord always reject us?

> Has he stopped loving us?
> Does his promise no longer stand?
> Has God forgotten to be merciful?
> Has anger taken the place of his compassion?
> …What hurts me most is this –
> that God is no longer powerful.
> (Psalm 77:7–10)

Yet now, I am more sure than ever that God never stops loving us, that his promises still stand, that he is infinitely compassionate and power belongs to him.

I had no instant answers for that hurting young man. Intimacy with God himself is the answer. The questions disappear in the face of the love and beauty of God. Any answer without knowing God is hollow and with God, in time, no answer seems necessary. Ruth Graham puts it this way:

> I lay my why
> Before your cross
> In worship kneeling
> My mind too numb for thought
> My heart beyond all feeling
> And worshipping
> Realise that I
> In knowing you
> Don't need a 'Why'.[7]

We were made to love him and be loved by him. Paul prayed that we would be rooted and grounded in that love. Rooted and grounded in him we cannot fail but to bloom again.

When I moved to my new home I bought two special plants, chosen for their names though I knew nothing of their blooms. One was a rose called Blessings, chosen at a time when I felt less blessed than ever in my whole life. The other was a rhododendron called Hallelujah, a word which

The Morning Chorus

had died on my lips in March 1985. For several winter months the rose displayed only bare stems and vicious thorns. Yet that plant contained, even then, the potential to produce a profusion of scented, delicate pink blooms. God knows that at times in our lives when we project only thorns the potential is still there for gentle fragrant beauty and all his gracious activity is designed to see us blossom once again, growing past the thorny barriers we create in our pain to become vulnerable beautiful people gracing his world.

From my bedroom window in summer my eyes can rest on that delicate pink rose growing against my window pane. It proclaims silently, 'God is a God of Blessings.'

I waited patiently for four years for tiny Hallelujah to flower. Each year its buds have burst to produce healthy green foliage. But no flowers. Now it is big enough and strong enough and I watch the flower buds forming, round and full. Praise has filled my heart and, when its petals finally open, it will just be an echo of what already is.

One of my favourite words in Scripture is 'It is finished' (John 19:30). With Garth's death I really believed my life was finished. Yet those words of Jesus are not a cry of defeat but a victory shout – '*It is finished*'. The shout of an athlete breaking the tape. The shout of victory: 'Look what has been done.' The powers of darkness were defeated, but there was more – much more. The resurrection followed. For me also he proclaimed, 'It is finished. I have defeated the darkness.'

Resurrection followed as he promised. He is the God of the living. Life is his business and rebuilding broken lives is what he does best.

From my comfortable perch on the verandah rail I hear the call of the tiny grey warbler, a crystal clear song my father named the unfinished symphony. There is more – much more – to enter into with God. I live an unfinished symphony but, with the little grey warbler, my heart sings again.

EPILOGUE

'We've chosen May the twelfth for our wedding.' My daughter Katrina is on the phone, excitedly telling her news. And me ... I'm suddenly aware of the significance of that weekend. It's the one Garth and I chose thirty-four years ago. My mind fills with images of the old mud-brick church perched on a hill in Naseby, the dazzling autumn landscape, friends and family – and that same excitement my daughter now shares with me.

I'm filled with joy that she and Tim should choose that weekend, but with surprise realise I've been widowed seventeen years. It seems like yesterday, but Katrina was ten then, and now here she is sharing her wedding plans with me… I pull myself back to the present and enter her excitement.

Grief catches us off balance at unexpected moments. Joy and pain mingle. I'm so glad they have chosen that weekend to marry. I'm also caught in a brief moment of longing.

When Garth's death left me and four children to re-arrange our lives, grief was a raw experience not unlike being submerged in a raging sea and when, with family, friends and God's help, I finally emerged onto the beach I wrote about my journey through that turbulent time from despair to hope.

The 'more – much more' that I concluded my story with has exceeded my dreams and expectations. It has been a wonderful journey.

God alone knew what the 'much more' would include: the opportunity to support grieving people, lead seminars, retreats, and parenting programmes, the chance to pursue study, lecture, teach and preach, my changing relationship to my adult children, the privilege of working with foster families through Open Home Foundation, the birth of another book, the joy of two precious grandchildren, and the celebration of a wedding (just to name a few) God has woven into my life what I learned through grief enabling me to use it in many ways.

When we moved to our home without Garth we asked God to build new memories for us. Ten years later when I sold our trusty Ford Econovan, I wrote a poem reflecting on its history: bike tours, when it was both larder and lodgings; its cavernous interior filled with musical instruments, or noisy youth group, bikes and dogs, wet towels and togs; the scrapes and dents from my learner drivers; the time it was belly up in the park (!) and all the fabulous holidays when transporting us to wilderness places or to family. God caught my attention, 'Look at the memories I have created.' Our prayers had been wonderfully answered. My heart overflowed with gratitude. Just as he promised our shattered lives were being restored.

Early in our grief, when we touched raw nerves in each other, I feared my children would want to leave home as soon as possible, never to return. But God has been at work, bathing our wounds, restoring our relationships, building a future and a hope. I treasure a hand made diary Katrina gave me – especially the words she wrote inside:

> I am realizing each day all the things you have done for me. You have sacrificed heaps for me and I am forever grateful. Thank you for giving me so much. You taught and teach me so much about life, love, relationships, service of God. You have taught me how to really love.
> I love you Mum.

Following the publication of *Shattered and Restored* I was invited to facilitate grief seminars in a number of churches around the country. I prayed that I might walk with others as my author friend Susan Lenzkes writes, 'Not with the spiked heels of advice and pat answers' but 'barefoot through the soul on ordinary days'[8] with sensitivity, respect and understanding.

I shared some of the tools God had shown me, gave some space for connecting with him, and some personal journaling time. God met those people in precious ways. What a joy to journey briefly with them. I am convinced God has the ultimate wisdom on grief. Effective counselling simply employs universal strategies God has already designed to facilitate healing.

Over the next few years I enjoyed leading workshops and retreats, exploring, among other things, grief, parenting, and intimacy with God. God had his ways of keeping my feet on the ground and my hand firmly in his. On one occasion, I was leading single parenting workshops at a conference with Ian Grant. Both Katrina and Aneta were present (the only teenagers) – grounded for a serious breech of rules just before the conference. I agonised about my credibility under the circumstances. But have you any idea how much credibility and rapport that gave me with those single parents? Again I learned God uses *all* things – even the death of my pride! And Aneta and Katrina had loads of fun in Ian Grant's workshops.

Single parenting highlighted for me the treasure of extended family, grandparents, aunts, uncles and cousins. My children's lives were all enriched by grandparents, now no longer with us. Sitting by Dad's hospital bed days before he died, I talked about his coming journey into the presence of God and asked Dad if he would tell Garth I loved him when he got there. Eyes sparkling from his aged and shrunken face, he replied. 'That won't be hard.' With Dad's death the two most significant men in my life were gone, but their impact remains – a gift from God that still shapes my life.

After Dad's death, to escape Naseby's icy winters Mum spent several weeks with us each year. Always cheerful and supportive, we loved her time with us. When frailty increased Mum chose to enter the rest home in Ranfurly, graciously accepting the changes. During our visits and phone calls she nourished us with her buoyancy and inner strength.

I awoke one morning, a poem for Mum forming in my head, acknowledging the skills, values and attitudes she had gifted to me. Entitled 'You Teach Me More than Ever Before', one snippet reads:

> You teach me strength is in the mind and spirit and emotions
> > in faith answering to God's direction
> That health is not measured…
> > in the heart that pumps
> > > but in the heart that loves…
> You are incredibly healthy.

God alone knew Mum would be forever free only days after receiving that poem. His timing was perfect. We gathered in the little church in Naseby where I first learned about God, where I married Garth and farewelled Dad, this time to celebrate Mum's life and to acknowledge that she would be home with her beloved Lord, with her husband and mine, in time for Christmas.

I fulfilled my commitment to lead the studies at a teenage camp the following week, up the Wanganui River. Mum had shared my enthusiasm and belief in the value of Christian camps, so I missed connecting with her afterwards to share what God had done. She had always shown intense interest in all I cared about. When her copy of *Shattered and Restored* was returned to me I found it stuffed full of news-clippings and reviews of my book, carefully saved by a proud mother.

If we weren't travelling south then we were heading north to see Garth's parents (no wonder the van clocked up so many memories). We celebrated their fifty years of marriage – and then sixty! Garth's mum died suddenly just before Christmas 2000. Ian was in England but the rest of us gathered with the McInnes clan to celebrate all she meant to each of us. Garth's dad died in February this year. Katrina and Tim had visited him just before leaving for England. Her email for his funeral concludes:

> You were the coolest granddad. You always made me feel really special. I loved talking to you in the garden and riding in your very cool car. You were always a lot of fun. It was hard seeing you last time. But I praise God that despite all the things you were going through, your personality and calm spirit showed through. Say hello to Grandma and Dad for me.

Epilogue

Now that I am a grandparent myself, I take my cue from those who filled this role so successfully for my children.

Thirteen years ago I escaped my noisy exuberant family to write the last chapter of *Shattered and Restored*. Today I write in a peaceful home. Now I can choose *my* kind of music, garden till dark, eat late, and store goodies in the pantry without them mysteriously disappearing! My fledglings have all flown. Jim left first, still smarting from his dad's death, restless in spirit, to try his hand at various cooking, fruit picking and building jobs. But God drew him back with cords of love. He went on a year's mission to the Czech republic where God revealed himself as Jim's heavenly Father. Love drew out the festering wound, and deep healing took place. It's always love that heals.

Love also opened Ian again to God, as he described at his baptism, age twenty. 'When Dad died I thought, "Well if that's the kind of God you are I don't want to know you." I shut my Bible and stopped praying. But God's people have gone on loving me regardless, until I can no longer resist God's love.' I'm grateful for healing love.

Deep gratitude has been tinged with momentary pain on special occasions. At each of my children's twenty-first birthday celebrations I acknowledged their dad and gave them something special that had been Garth's. Ian, Katrina and Jim's baptisms were celebrations where Garth would have joyfully officiated. Katrina's graduation from Otago University, wearing with pride and tears her dad's preaching gown, was a wonderful occasion. Jim's recent graduation from Bible College and an invitation to lecture there would have filled his dad with pride. My grandchildren have brought me great joy, but just occasionally I'm saddened by the thought that they will never know their granddad.

On 12 May 2001 Katrina and Tim celebrated their wedding. Ian came from England for this wonderful family time. Katrina shared, 'Mum and Dad would have been married thirty-four years today.' Yes, we shed tears, but they were healing tears rich with memory and gratitude for the all-encompassing grace of God.

With gratitude I've watched God direct each of my adult children as they engage their faith with the world. Over the years Ian has caved, climbed, kayaked and skied most of New Zealand and developed his skill in working with youth. While overseas, his faith, together with his passion for disadvantaged youth, under-girded his work as Youth Development Manager for Lakeside Outdoor Centre, England, and is now reflected in his work as Operations Director for Adventure Specialties in Auckland.

Jim has an ever-deepening relationship with God. As Director of Youth for Christ, Nelson, he has a passion to see young people discipled in Jesus, because he knows it's their lifeblood, healing and hope.

Aneta brings love and commitment to her relationship with Bevan, support for his fibreglass business in Wanaka, the fruit of the Spirit to parenting Tayla and Avon, and friendliness to everyone.

Katrina reaches people with her contagious laughter and enjoys facilitating worship. As a physical education teacher at Nelson High School, she was always looking for ways to help hurting young people. Currently she and Tim are working in London with frequent excursions to explore more of God's world.

Just as my children have experienced new things so have I. In 1993 I began working for Open Home Foundation, a wonderful Christian child and family support service. I have been employed there for ten years now, recruiting, supporting and training foster families who reflect the love of God to children in need. I marvel at how God has woven together all my life experiences for this task but especially my journey through grief, enlarging my heart for hurting families and deepening my understanding. I feel the heartbeat of God for families. It is the same as his heartbeat for my family – to bring healing and restoration.

During my own children's journey from heartbreak to restoration I became aware of the scarcity of help for young people experiencing profound loss. Teenagers I met while leading studies on Christian camps, were often hiding silent grief behind masks of joviality. I invited some young people to tell how they experienced grief and grew through it with God's help. My aim was to produce a book offering other young people hope for the hard times. It was my great privilege to work with nine New Zealanders and three Australians as they wrote their stories, and to shed tears, admire their courage, and celebrate their growth.

Epilogue

Finding a publisher was difficult. Only the writers' enthusiasm and an oft-repeated word from God, 'hang in there', kept me going. By God's grace I discovered Castle Publishing, whose mission is to support New Zealand Christian writers. Guided by a 'God nudge', I invited friends to pre-order one or more copies of the book at twice the retail price to sponsor publication (what audacity, and hardly a bargain!). The response was overwhelming. Our book, the result of a huge team effort, was launched with thanksgiving in 2001. *A Grip on Grief* is now into its second printing. More importantly it is fulfilling our vision – to help young people through grief.

Recently I've enjoyed training to be a Spiritual Director, so that I can give to others that same loving attention I appreciate when I explore my relationship with God, especially through turbulent times.

Today, pausing in my writing, I look out on my wintry garden. The blackbirds are devouring the remaining apples, and the rose 'Blessings' has one late bloom – a splash of colour amongst tired leaves. The scene reminds me of a recent season in my life when breast cancer was discovered. This news ushered in some dark days. But darkness and light are the same to God; both are inhabited by him. Could he colour this new season? The grief was real. I recognised its familiar voice. 'There's no future.' 'It's all downhill from here.' I felt old and ugly like the leaves on my rose bush. But having previously traversed the landscape of grief, I was more aware of the destructive thought-patterns leading to depression. I knew the importance of both being honest with God about my feelings, and having my heart open to receive his comfort and love 'in the midst'. At the end of busy work days before surgery I wrote to God to get in touch with my feelings, to release fear, dislodge negative thoughts and rebuild my shattered self-image. Writing drained my confused emotions, making space for God to plant his gentle Word in my spirit, and helping me move from fear to trust.

God came with gifts to colour even this season: a skilful Christian surgeon, a good prognosis, caring district nurses, visits from friends and work colleagues, and the help of my sister Shona and Aneta who livened up my home, filling my days with laughter – sometimes at my expense when I got tubes tangled around furniture, forgetting I had 'attachments' to lug around! Winter gave way, as winter always does; energy has returned, hope is again restored, my trust in God deepened and my storehouse of treasures enlarged.

One weekend last September, before I had a whisper of cancer (and God knew that's the way it should be), my family gathered to farewell Tim and Katrina. With hilarity they sorted through stuff forgotten since childhood – collections of postcards, erasers, seventies garb, homemade school bags and scratchy recordings of budding McInnes musicians. Then out came the Monopoly and the day was capped off by an early Christmas dinner. Memories, one of God's great blessings, sustained me a month later as I faced new medical terminology and procedures.

At Christmas Jim and Ian came home to paint the roof. I so enjoyed their company. I thought back to the years following Garth's death when our relationships were strained. God is definitely in the restoration business, it's what he does best – and my roof looks great too.

I'm reminded that in God's economy life is a series of endings followed by new beginnings, just like Easter, and still the old hymn sung at Garth's funeral rings true, 'God will repay from his own fullness all he takes away'.

That fullness includes Bevan and Tim, each bringing their special personalities and my precious grandchildren, Tayla and Avon who believe Nana is wired to read stories at 6.00 a.m. or any other time, and they are right! On a recent visit to Wanaka they tiptoed in very early, snuggling their cold feet into my bed and I read to them *The Velveteen Rabbit*, about toys in a nursery. I like the skin horse's reflection on what is 'real':

> "Real isn't how you are made," said the skin horse. "You become. It takes a long time. That's why it doesn't happen to people who break easily, or have sharp edges, or have to be carefully kept. Generally by the time you are real, most of your hair has been loved off, and your eyes drop out and you get loose in the joints and very shabby. But these things don't matter at all, because once you are Real you can't be ugly except to people who don't understand."[9]

That's very consoling as I clock up my sixtieth birthday, knowing that those who love me, God included, are not concerned if I'm wearing a trifle 'shabby'.

Before I even contemplate the 'loose in the joints' stage, I've enjoyed many of the great walks with friends, strolling the cool bush clad valleys, puffing along expansive alpine peaks, wandering along shimmering shore lines, loving the awe inspiring beauty. The contrasts in the landscape mirror my life's journey. My experience is that God inhabits *every* landscape and *every* season – each beautiful in its own way.

This new season, turning sixty, was marked by a celebration at Naseby, planned by my children on a glorious winter's day. It was a time to recollect, as the Israelites did at the stone altars built to remember God's activity. The remembering gives inspiration for the journey. My life remains, as I wrote before and the grey warbler reminds me still, '"an unfinished symphony". There is always more to enter into with God.' When I wrote those words thirteen years ago I had no idea what these years would bring. My God promises and delivers 'life in all its fullness' summer and winter, valleys and mountains, sorrow and joy all filled with meaning and enriched by his presence.

REFERENCES

1. C. S. Lewis, *A Grief Observed* (Faber and Faber, 1967), p. 7.

2. ibid., p. 29.

3. Morton Kelsey, *The Other Side of Silence: A Guide to Meditation* (SPCK), p. 77.

4. ibid., p. 156.

5. Lewis, op. cit., p. 38.

6. Patty Kennedy, *Just Like You Promised* (© 1982 Mercy Publishing, Administered in Australasia by Scripture in Song).

7. Ruth Graham, *It's My Turn* (Fleming H Revell), p. 169.

8. Susan Lenzkes, 'A Friend in Need', *Silver Pen for Cloudy Days* (Daybreak Books, 1987), p. 50.

9. Margery Williams, *The Velveteen Rabbit* (Mammoth Edition, an imprint of Egmont Children's Books, 1992).

ALSO BY ELSA McINNES

Elsa McInnes presents twelve true-life stories, written by Australian and New Zealand young people, about their experiences of intense loss.

Elsa contributes chapters on: 'The Truth About Loss', 'Where is God When It All Goes Wrong?', 'Is There Life After Grief?' and 'If You Get Stuck – Where to Go for Help'. Includes an index to grief themes.

A GRIP ON GRIEF will help you through the worst times, and help others understand what it means to lose someone close.

"This is not a sappy collection of clichés about life and death. Here you will find real answers on how to deal with grief positively, without denying its tremendous power to shock us, distort our feel for reality and wound us in our deepest parts.' – Ian Grant

For more information on this and other Castle titles, please email: orders@castlepublishing.biz

RECOMMENDED READING

The Monster in the Mirror
By Karen Mackintosh

The firsthand story of how one woman took on the eating disorder monster and won.

All This and the Moon
By Bernadene Erasmus

The heartfelt and gripping story of a woman who wanted to make a big difference in the lives of Down Syndrome youth.

Direct Encounter
By Joyce Mitchell

Laugh and cry with Joyce Mitchell as she recounts her life story and the challenges of pursuing true purpose and fulfilment in every area of life.

Shooting the Globe
By Maurice Harvey

A fascinating and entertaining book that takes the reader closer to the human soul of some of the world's most isolated places and hotspots of recent history.